OUR DAY
IN MAY

THE INSIDE STORY OF ST JOHNSTONE FC'S
FIRST MAJOR TROPHY WIN IN 130 YEARS

OUR DAY
IN MAY

THE INSIDE STORY OF ST JOHNSTONE FC'S
FIRST MAJOR TROPHY WIN IN 130 YEARS

ED HODGE

First published in Great Britain in 2015 by
ARENA SPORT
An imprint of Birlinn Limited
West Newington House
10 Newington Road
Edinburgh
EH9 1QS

www.arenasportbooks.co.uk

ISBN: 9781909715301
eBook ISBN: 9780857908599

British Library Cataloguing-in-Publication Data
A catalogue record for this book is available on request from the
British Library.

Designed and typeset by Polaris Publishing, Edinburgh

Printed and bound by Bell & Bain Ltd, Glasgow

CONTENTS

For all the Perth Saints, near and far

ACKNOWLEDGEMENTS

2014. WHEN WILL Perthshire see your like again? Gleneagles sparkled under the Ryder Cup spotlight to an audience of millions; Blairgowrie put on a super show for the Junior equivalent with the local Amateur champion pulling on the European jersey; and the local football team just so happened to lift their first major trophy in their 130-year history. It truly was a momentous sporting year for the Big County.

I'm privileged to have been a part of it all, and have relished the opportunity to write two books on the two sports subjects easily the closest to my heart. Having worked with The Gleneagles Hotel and Arena Sport, an imprint of Birlinn Ltd, to pen my first book in 2013, *Jewel in the Glen: Gleneagles, Golf and The Ryder Cup*, and updated the edition post-Europe's triumph in September 2014, the idea of writing a book on St Johnstone's stunning Scottish Cup triumph refused to leave me.

I've been hooked on Saints for over quarter of a century since growing up in Braco, Perthshire. Having attended a couple of games at Muirton Park, it was my dad, Kenneth, who set the wheels in motion for my continued passion for the Perth side when he took me along to the first-ever game at McDiarmid Park on 19 August 1989. In the UK's first all-seated, purpose-built football stadium, St Johnstone defeated Clydebank 2-1. Aged 11, I still vividly recall that win and the bumper crowd, with the Cherrybank Inn in Perth soon becoming a regular haunt with dad and a few of his former work colleagues before games. Those were wonderful days for a teenage fan, with the title-defining 3-1 victory over Airdrie on a sun-kissed afternoon holding a special memory. Indeed, other than the Scottish Cup final win, it's my favourite game. I remember dad and I then headed down to Somerset Park to witness Saints seal the First Division Championship at Ayr United and enjoy a victory handshake from Alex Totten on his lap of honour.

In the top flight, who can forget that 5-0 rout of Aberdeen and sell-out clashes with the Old Firm. At the time, Gordon Bannerman's fine book, *Saints Alive*, was published and it planted a seed for the dream of one day writing my own. Paul Sturrock and Sandy Clark went on to enjoy good spells at the club before, in more recent times, Owen Coyle, Derek McInnes and Steve Lomas returned Saints to a position of standing within Scottish football. For Tommy Wright to end the pain of all those semi-final defeats and achieve the seemingly impossible was simply astonishing; an achievement the club can treasure for ever more. On May 17, 2014, I admit to being as nervous as I've ever been at a sporting event. It was our time – and we simply had to take it. How I enjoyed the celebrations, especially the Sunday parade in Perth with my young children on my shoulders.

Thanks to my sports journalism background going back to the late 1990s, I've been delighted to cover Saints over the years, speaking to players and management, and have continued to follow them closely while working for the Scottish Golf Union (SGU) since 2011. Indeed, I've witnessed, first hand, the quality of Callum Davidson's golf and continue to badger him to tee it up in the Scottish Amateur Championship one day!

The year 2014 was a busy one for me, especially with family commitments, and it was only towards the end of the calendar year that I felt in a position to progress the Saints cup final book idea – despite the reservations of my wife, Iona! Having pestered and persuaded Peter Burns, the sports editor at Arena Sport, after receiving support from Tommy and Callum, I pitched the book concept to Steve Brown and Roddy Grant at the club. The rest, as they say, is history.

Ultimately, I wanted the players and management to tell the story through their own eyes on how they progressed through all five rounds to achieve the most notable success in the club's history. To do so, I've spoken with over 20 players and the backroom team of Tommy, Callum and Alex Cleland. My huge thanks go to Tommy, Callum and the Perthshire Advertiser's Gordon Bannerman, now a close journalist colleague, for helping me track the players down, past and present. It's been a joy to hear all their memories on the cup victory and how much it has meant to each and every one of them. From the captain Dave Mackay to the cup final goal heroes Steven Anderson and Steven MacLean to the season's talisman Stevie May, I thank you all.

It was then a case of quickly piecing the 'jigsaw' together to produce a publication that everyone at the club and all the fans could look back on proudly for years to come – with the fitting publication date of May 17 to mark the one-year cup anniversary. It's thus, hopefully, a story for any St Johnstone fan to treasure, a story told by those who are heroes forever, a story about a long-cherished dream finally coming true; a story about our 'wee' club finally enjoying its big day. Only a supporter of a smaller club will understand how that feels.

Gordon, Keith Rose, formerly of Gleneagles Golf Publishing Ltd, and SGU colleague Janette Dewar rallied round to help with the proof reading, while Perth freelance and club photographer Graeme Hart kindly offered his images for use in the book gratis. I'm indebted to their support. Thanks also to the local band, The Shrugs, for allowing the use of their lyrics at the start of all eight chapters. How their cup final song was lustily sung in the days before and after cup glory. Paul Smith and Ross Cunningham have been a great source of support at McDiarmid Park, while owner Geoff Brown was kind enough to grant me an interview for the foreword and the chairman, Steve, for the postscript. Thanks, finally, to those who offered me some fan contributions at the end of the book, notably Stuart Cosgrove, Colin McCredie and Eve Muirhead.

Ultimately, the book is about giving something back to the club. Having enjoyed some wonderful memories from over 25 years supporting Saints, I wanted the club to benefit from book sales and royalties will go to the club's youth development programme. If that helps unearth another Stevie May over time, then, of course, we'll all be delighted.

Tommy and his team consistently use the word 'fate' during the cup run. 'Belief' is another word repeatedly mentioned. It all conspired to produce those triumphant scenes on May 17, 2014. The day the Saints finally went marching in, and a date none of us will ever forget. Enjoy the read.

Ed Hodge

FOREWORD

BY GEOFF BROWN, OWNER

I'LL ALWAYS LOOK back on 2014 with fondness – we all will. Having gone through triple heart bypass surgery, it's also a year that put things in perspective for me, and made me think about what is important. There is more to life than football, after all. Admittedly, it didn't feel like that on 17 May! It was a great chance to win the Scottish Cup – and we took it. It was a super day and I was so proud for everyone connected with the club, just as I am to write this foreword for the club's official cup final book.

It's funny looking back, at times. One of my best memories from the Scottish Cup run is actually from the semi-final. Alistair McCracken was St Johnstone's doctor for over 20 years and is a super guy. He practiced in Kinross, did a lot of club medicals and was a real fanatic for the team. For the Aberdeen semi-final, he was over in the Western Isles on holiday and went into a pub to watch the game. Aberdeen went 1-0 up and out he went, away for a walk with his dog. He eventually came back in and it was 1-1. So he sat down to watch the game again and then up popped Stevie May with the second goal. The next thing, they threw him out of the pub! I enjoyed myself after that win, but not to that degree!

After our 4-0 defeat to Aberdeen in the League Cup semi-final, I think there were a lot of people not exactly looking forward to the next semi-final with the Dons. I went with the fans to the first game at Tynecastle and the rain was coming down as we were leaking goals. We trekked back to the bus, heads down, nobody speaking, it was a real fans' feeling. I admit I was apprehensive going to Ibrox to face them again – but it ended up a marvellous day. I know the Aberdeen chairman, Stewart Milne, exceptionally

Geoff Brown with his wife, Joyce, and the Scottish Cup. *Graeme Hart*

well and he came onto our team bus and said 'congratulations' after our win, which I thought was a great gesture.

I effectively introduced Stewart to Derek McInnes, so every time we met I said 'when am I getting my agent's fee?' When they went on to win the League Cup, I texted him again and said 'well done... and when am I getting my agent's fee?' Wonderfully, the following morning there was a case of champagne sitting on my office table. It was from Stewart with a wee note, 'enjoy the champagne and you're certainly not getting an agent's fee'!

So I still enjoy having a bit of banter with guys I used to see regularly but, of course, things have moved on for me after being hands-on at the club from 1986 to 2011. I was born and bred in Perth – in fact I was born in St Johnstoun's Nursing Home. I've always been a football fanatic. I didn't always go along every Saturday to watch Saints, with family commitments and such like, but they were always in my life. Coming into the club in '86, there was nobody else! The previous board had tried all and sundry to see who would be interested. Little did my wife, Joyce, know what I was getting myself involved in! The first horse I bought was in 1986, as well. And I've had GS Brown since 1970, so it's been a busy old time over the years, but good fun.

I'm pleased the club has been, and continues to be, run properly. If you don't manage properly, you've no chance. At some clubs it's been absolutely crazy. Look at what has happened with the likes of Rangers, Gretna, Hearts and Livingston over the years. There were TV programmes about the Gretna 'dream' and their climb up the leagues, but where else could it have gone? You don't go spending money like they did – nobody can do that. Many believe money is the motivator, but that's not the case when you are running a football club. Did that therefore make our cup triumph sweeter for me? Probably. But what felt nicer for me was that over the years reporters said we weren't spending and had no ambition. For years, it was the board's fault because we didn't spend money. But you only had to look at the accounts of other clubs to understand why. A lot of situations were false economies, accruing debt. We have run a good, prudent club, and that pleases me, although that's self praise which, I don't like!

At times it has been difficult, since stepping away to let my son, Steve, come in as chairman in 2011, but I made a conscious decision. I'm a great believer that when you do that you have to stand back completely and not look over people's shoulders. You have to allow them to get on with it. I don't think they have missed me somehow, having won a cup and been in Europe three times in a row, so it can't be said that if I was there we could have been more successful! Joyce is an elder of the church and she has a job getting me to go. She says 'I'll go to my church, you go to yours (McDiarmid Park)'. I enjoy going to the games as a 'fan' now. But there is a wee problem with me in the directors' box, because I'll shout what I'm thinking. I've never been shy in showing those sorts of emotions!

When I decided to leave as chairman, Derek McInnes had left and there was a new manager coming in. To me, there were also younger people coming through the club. The first manager that I employed was Alex Totten and he was close to my age group, so I could relate to that. When people you are employing are younger than your own family, you know that's the time to go. When Steve was on the board, he really only had a small insight into what was going on at the club, so he got quite a fright when he was asked to get on with it! It's an entirely different experience when you are in charge. I'm very pleased for him. Things have gone well, yet they can just as easily go poorly if you look at the downturn at Motherwell, for example, after their high finishes in previous seasons. At no time can you get complacent.

While Owen Coyle took us to that step of almost getting back to the top flight and enjoyed some great days, Derek McInnes did a superior job as he changed quite a lot at the club and got us out of the First Division. Steve Lomas then kept things going. I don't know Tommy Wright that well, but I always saw him as being a big, canny type of individual with principle. He is one of those guys you would be quite happy going to dinner with. I knew, probably like most fans did, that he had a good squad going into the cup-winning season. Stevie May started the season exceptionally well, he was a real spark for the club, but they all did well. Defensively we were well organised and we didn't look like we would be beaten on many occasions that season, so you are always hopeful of doing something in the cups.

We had suffered all those semi-final defeats, but they were against good sides and our luck had to change at some point. Indeed, when we beat Aberdeen in the semi-finals it was the first time we had beaten a club above us in the league in the last four in recent times. You can have cup runs and meet lower league sides, but we had lost semis to the likes of Celtic, Rangers, Hibs and Motherwell and they were ahead of us in the league at the time.

I'll always remember it being rather quiet when we met at the club on the morning of the cup final. After all those semi-final defeats, we knew it was a big day, so there were nerves amongst us. Mind you, I was scheduled to go in for the triple heart bypass, so the cup final was nothing compared to what I was to go through! The team came out and they looked up for it. The fans were up for it, and I just didn't see Dundee United on the day being able to beat us. We had beaten them three times previously without conceding a goal, so why should we have gone out with anything less than the belief that we could do it? If our guys turned up on the day, we were capable of winning, and so it proved.

A lot of noise was still made about our cup win being a big shock, against all the odds, but we had finished in the top six for three successive seasons, and Rangers were out of the equation. We should have been knocking at the door to win a trophy – and we did. Personally, I didn't see it as being something that was extraordinary. It was extraordinary in terms of the day out, but not in the sense of winning it. We beat Aberdeen in the semi-final and continued our great record against Dundee United during the season to win the final. It was tremendous seeing the smiles on all the fans' faces at the end. The real reward you get at a football club is seeing other people smiling. If you are winning, it makes everyone feel good. And, of course, we'd love to see more of those 15,000 fans who attended the final come more regularly to games at Perth. People put so much work into the club as volunteers and the club deserves more support. We would all like to see the core fan base higher and I know the club is trying everything they can to achieve that.

It was a proud day to see all that blue and white at Celtic Park, but Sunday in Perth was just unbelievable. I couldn't believe it when the bus turned up the High Street! The number of people! I've stayed in Perth all my days and I've never ever seen anything close to the numbers that were there that day. It was simply unbelievable. I remember passing Boots and fans were streaming in the front door of the shop and out the back. I'm sure they were delighted! I recognised a few faces and was hugging people and signing autographs. It was unreal. Although, I'm not sure we would have passed any health and safety test with the number of people on the open top bus!

Personally, I knew there were tougher times to come as it was back at the end of February that I was getting chest pains. It was around the end of April when things were agreed with my doctor and I went in on 14 July for the operation the following day. Saints' Europa League game away to Lucerne was on the 17th, and most of my family travelled while I was lying sawn from top to bottom in a hospital bed in Edinburgh. However, it brings me to conclude on another wee story...

I had been waiting about seven weeks to go into hospital and I finally got word to go for pre-tests. That took two-and-a-half-hours, before I ended up in a consultancy room. I got talking to Doctor Daisy Sandeman. She knew that I knew Dr Andrew Flapan, a Cardiologist, who has done a lot of work for the football club. 'Are you interested in football?' she said. 'I don't know, but I own a club', I stated. She said that she and her husband were season ticket holders at Celtic. 'I'll do a deal with you,' I remarked. 'And what would that be?' she replied. 'The deal is quite simple. You get me in here as quickly as possible and you get me out even quicker.' She looked at me. 'If you can do that, what I'll do is take you and your husband to the boardroom at McDiarmid Park for the St Johnstone game against Celtic at the start of the season'. She said 'would you do that?' 'Of course,' I said.

From that moment, I never saw her again until the Sunday morning when I was lying in bed after the operation. 'You are getting on well, Mr Brown,' she said. 'I'm not getting on that well, I'm still here,' I replied. It was about 11am, so another patient and I went for a walk around the hospital, before Daisy appeared again shortly before 2pm. She said 'you know that deal we have?' 'Yes'. 'Well, my husband and I are going to Australia for three weeks so I won't be able to come to Perth. But, listen, I'll keep my end of the deal and you can go home now if you want.' In hospitals, you can usually only get out on a Friday or a Monday so I said 'right, fine, I'm off, thanks very much'.

Given they couldn't make the first Celtic game, I phoned her up a couple of weeks before Saints were playing them in February this year and she and her husband both duly came along. They met Eric Reilly, the finance director at Celtic, who I know well, and they were kindly asked along for the Saints game at Celtic in early March. They are season ticket holders at Celtic, but how many get through their front door? So Doctor Daisy was delighted and they looked forward to it. In between time, her husband runs a small wine company and they had been in Australia for that very reason. She duly sent some wine to the club as a thank you, so I thought I was doing rather well out of things!

Of course, she was sitting beside me at Celtic Park in March and, with 15 minutes to go, I took her hand and said 'look,

Daisy, this is not about life and death. This is only a game and if you're going to get beat, you're going to get beat!' I was rubbing it in, sitting next to Celtic season ticket holders as we won 1-0. And it all stemmed from me going into hospital and making a deal. I wouldn't think many people do that! Health and happiness, that's how I'll remember the year 2014. And, for everyone connected with Saints, I'm sure it was one of the best years of their lives.

I have to conclude with thanking all my family and the volunteers and fans who stood by St Johnstone in the bad times. The Scottish Cup win is for you.

1

BUILDING BLOCKS

Just another normal day,
Another girlfriend gone astray,
She wanted more, she slammed the door,
And threw my Saints scarf on the floor,
She said, 'will you, will you please
Sort out your priorities?'
I agreed.
So I bought a season ticket.

'Fair Maid'
The Shrugs
(Scottish Cup Final Song)

ON 16 APRIL 2011, St Johnstone Football Club contested their fifth semi-final in a major cup competition in just over four years. For a small, provincial club with limited resources that was a feat in itself. The work of Owen Coyle and Derek McInnes had helped form capable, well-drilled teams, none more so than in one-off games. The 2-0 victory for Coyle's side at Ibrox in the League Cup quarter-final of November 2006 was a case in point, the first time Rangers had been knocked out of a cup tournament by a lower league side at home, as Steven Milne struck a stunning double.

Of course, like the four previous semi-finals, the match in April 2011 resulted in defeat. At Hampden Park, it was game over for Saints against Motherwell before half-time. It was the club's eighth Scottish Cup semi-final defeat in a row, that elusive final place still out of reach. More heartache and more pain; especially for those who had suffered the agony on more than one occasion.

Indeed, despite reaching the League Cup finals of 1969 and 1998, under Willie Ormond and Sandy Clark respectively, there was a nagging feeling in the present day about whether the club could break the psychological barrier of the pressurised last-four stage. Yes, the club had won the lower-tier Challenge Cup, their first national cup success in 2007, and yes, were performing admirably, re-establishing themselves back in Scotland's top flight after a seven-year absence thanks to First Division title success under McInnes in 2009, but the pain of each semi-final defeat was only becoming more pronounced.

With McInnes departing to Bristol City in October 2011, a new era began at Perth under the former West Ham and Northern Ireland midfielder Steve Lomas. Alongside him was his countryman, Tommy Wright, the 31-capped former goalkeeper and ex-Lisburn Distillery manager. In his first season, Lomas guided the club to a top-six finish and into the Europa League, both for the first time since 1999. He repeated the feat the following season, at one point sitting second in the table behind Celtic and finishing third overall, as Saints fans basked in wonderful, notable days. Having been linked with a host of English clubs, Lomas took the bold move to take over at Millwall, West Ham's fierce rivals, in June 2013. Wright opted against joining him, instead jumping into the Perth hot-seat. Light-hearted banter soon began between Wright and Perth chairman, Steve Brown. 'Of course, you'll have to win the cup,' said Brown, in reference to what the club had already achieved in previous seasons. Wright said he would. It was a little joke, but they kept repeating it...

Tommy Wright, Manager, 51

I knew Steve Lomas, we were friends but not close. I'm a lot older than him, but I worked with him at Manchester City and I played with him at Northern Ireland. He worked briefly at Norwich when I was goalkeeping coach, so we kept in touch and, since 2009, he had started doing Sky games and I was giving him info on Irish League clubs. He had asked me a couple of times 'if I got a job, would I come with him?' I said 'yes, no problem'. Out of the blue I got a call, at the end of October 2011, and he said 'I'm going for this job, I might get it, and I want you to be my assistant.' Part of it as well, was that I was able to be his assistant and goalkeeping coach, which helped keep the costs down. He got the job and I moved over, coming over to St Johnstone on 4 November. Lisburn Distillery were very good, released me out of my contract, and that was it.

I was settled at home but I still wanted to work in full-time football, which was one reason why I went to Norwich. Initially, when I finished playing, I moved back home and I worked as a youth development officer for the Irish Football Association, before I got a job at Limavady United and did reasonably well there. They were bottom of the league and we ended up seventh and fifth in my two years. I left to join Ballymena United and got them into the top six for the first time in quite a few years, brought through young players and did reasonably well there, too. I got an opportunity to go to Norwich, but my father-in-law took ill and my wife, Anne, and I turned it down, but the opportunity came again and I went to Norwich as goalkeeping coach, working under Glenn Roeder. When Glenn got the sack in January 2009 they wanted to keep me on, but I was uncomfortable at staying so I eventually agreed a package to leave and went home where my former team-mate Michael O'Neill took me down to Shamrock Rovers as his goalie coach. But Northern Ireland is part-time football, even though at Ballymena I was full-time because I was running a community programme during the day. You only train two nights a week, so I had that burning ambition to get back into full-time football, either as a coach, manager or goalie coach. With football tightening its finances, assistant and goalie coach gave me an extra string to my bow, and probably helped Steve sell taking me to St Johnstone. But the decision to come was tough inasmuch as I was settled at home, with my house, and at Distillery. We had won the Irish League Cup in 2011 and we had come through a lot as they were in administration – we had basically kept the club together. After they released me from my contract, I think the biggest factor was just leaving home again after being back for the guts of 10 to 11 years. When I was at Norwich, I popped back and forward, I was based in Ireland, because in football you never know. Anne had no problem with it, coming to St Johnstone, she was delighted, but it was still a bit of a wrench to be leaving home again. But I came here and settled very quickly, working with Steve.

In fact, my decision not to go with Steve (to Millwall) is probably one of the best decisions I've ever made. People won't believe it, but it was the easiest decision I've ever had to make. Steve had this desire to get away down south again and I wasn't as keen on that. We'd discussed it before and I was never keen. The Millwall thing came up, but I wanted to stay and see what would happen. At the end, he did want to get away. He phoned me up and said 'Millwall have come in for me and I want you to come with me.' I said 'no'. He asked me three more times and I said 'no'. My main reasons were that I've always lived in places like Newcastle, Manchester and Nottingham in my playing days. They are not huge cities, I was able to lead a simple life, get on with things, no hustle and bustle, and London... well, I just know I definitely wouldn't have settled in London.

From a professional point of view, I told him Millwall was the wrong club. That was my biggest concern – that we would go down there and you would be out on your ear within less than a season. I know the hatred between Millwall and West Ham. So I didn't go and that's the last I've heard from Steve, which is disappointing. But I was left in limbo because I informed the chairman that I wasn't going. I was under contract, and we had a meeting. He basically asked me 'what are we going to do now?'

I said I would like to be considered for the job and the rest is history...

Frazer Wright, Defender, 35
It just took the boys a wee while to stop calling him Tommy... and 'gaffer' instead.

Tommy Wright
I felt confident I had built up a relationship with the board and the chairman. I was the go-between at times between Steve and the chairman. That probably helped me, building up a relationship, which probably in normal circumstances wouldn't have happened. I think the chairman knew what type of person I was, he knew that the players would be comfortable with me, he knew the transition would be seamless, he knew what he was going to get from me. In goalkeeping terms, I could have been looked upon as a safe pair of hands to take on the job. I think what the chairman liked as well was that I understood the club. I knew there were going to be cuts to the budget that season, but I understood why it had to be done because it's about the future of the club. I understand the workings of the club – that we can't always just get from A to B as quickly as possible, we have to make little steps of improvement. The deal was done very quickly and I was appointed.

Callum Davidson, Assistant Manager, 38
The assistant manager role came about basically when I was on holiday and I got a phone call on 8 June, roughly. I had been unemployed for eight days, for the first time in my life after finishing my playing career at Saints. I knew Steve had gone to Millwall and Tommy asked if I wanted to be his assistant. It was a good call on holiday, but at the same time I was instructed to fly back from Portugal, leaving my wife and kids. That went down well! Tommy was in Portugal on holiday as well, but we flew back

and signed the deals and did the press. It was all good. Tommy and I talked about the season ahead, with the big Europa League qualifier against Rosenborg coming up, planning everything and what players we were looking to sign.

Tommy Wright

Choosing my backroom team was a hard thing to do. The natural progression may have been that Alex Cleland stepped up to be assistant manager because Callum had just finished playing. But I had seen Callum work with the Under-20s, got to know him really well, and I went for him as my assistant with Alex as my first-team coach and Under-20 coach. But the three of us work together, along with the other staff. When we're sitting working together as a three, there are no real titles.

Alex Cleland, Under-20s & First-team Coach, 44

It was Derek McInnes who first brought me to the club from Inverness in the summer of 2009. Inverness had been relegated to the First Division and we were told they were disbanding the Under-20 side, which I managed. It was a shame as we had a good side up there with exciting players, like Nick Ross, Graeme Shinnie and Stuart Armstrong. People forget Armstrong was an Inverness player who came through their youth set up. All the money had to go into the Inverness first team to try and get them back up, so I lost my job. I had said I would try to look after some players, so I phoned round all my contacts, including Derek who had taken Saints up to the top flight that year. As it turned out, Derek asked me if I would be interested in taking their Under-20s for the next season as he was looking for a coach. He knew I had been taking the Under-20s for three or four years (at Livingston and Inverness), and he needed somebody with experience who he could trust, so I took the job. It was an easy decision. At that time, Saints had young lads like Liam Caddis, Alexander Clark and Stevie May, a good core. They had a very successful season at Under-17 level the season before I took them for the Under-20s. It was an exciting new chapter for me because it was the first time St Johnstone Under-19s were going to be represented in the top flight. It was great to go back and work with Derek and Tony Docherty. I knew Tony from working against him when he was youth coach at Dundee United and I knew Derek well, having played at Rangers together.

When Steve and Tommy first came to Perth, my role was to give them as much information as I could, because they were relatively unaware about Scottish football and the players. They saw that I needed a fresh challenge so they got me more involved with the first-team, but I could still oversee the Under-20s. I was delighted when Tommy came and said to me he was bringing in Callum as his assistant manager and I was to be first-team / Under-20s coach. He wanted Callum to take the Under-20s, so I just assisted Callum with anything he needed, as they were new roles for him and he had a lot on his plate. I was delighted to help him along the way, and we bounced ideas off each other. If he was doing more with the first-team, I would go and do more with the Under-20s, that's how it's worked. Between the three of us, and Alistair Stevenson (youth development coach), I think we have the balance right. We all work together.

Callum Davidson
I didn't think an opportunity like assistant would come as quickly as that. I was delighted as it is difficult when you're out of the game to get back in, so I was very fortunate. I was one of the older ones when I retired, so there is quite a big gap in age difference with the squad. Frazer Wright is probably the closest one. I had taken training before, Derek McInnes started that off, letting me take training on a Monday, so that kind of started me on that path. I also helped coach the Under-20s which was a good experience and helped me a lot.

Brian Easton, Defender, 27

Callum has helped a lot. He's been a nice go-between for the manager and the dressing room. He's got a good rapport with the boys.

Tommy Wright

Going into my first season in charge (2013-14), I knew the club's history. They had recently been in semi-finals of the cup, with Derek and Owen. I was aware of that. And, because of the size of the club, I was aware of the importance of cup runs. They offer a great opportunity to get silverware and increase revenue the more you progress. But we had lost almost 30 goals from the squad ahead of the season. Murray Davidson at that stage had gone, Liam Craig had gone, Rowan Vine had gone, and Gregory Tade had gone. Ok, Murray came back, but Tade had a year's option, said he would sign it, and then did a U-turn which can happen. I think the important thing for me was letting Stevie May know that he would get a chance. My first meeting with the players was quite simple, I said 'I'm in the job, I'm not the assistant manager anymore and you've got to respect that. I'll have decisions to make, I'm not afraid to make big decisions and people will be left out, as my only concern is the team. It's my No 1 priority. I'm quite fortunate to be able to walk into a dressing room where I know I can trust every one of you as players, and as individuals. You may all trust me as an individual, so I'll hopefully gain your trust as a manager over a period of time.' That was important with the squad, it was important with people like Stevie May to say 'Bang, you're going nowhere, you aren't going out on loan again, I'll give you an opportunity to play and it's up to you'. He said 'You give me the opportunity, gaffer, and I'll score goals.'

I watched Stevie when he was on loan with Hamilton and he had bright yellow boots and the ponytail and he was getting dog's abuse at Raith. He was shooting from everywhere and he was getting pelters. He almost had an air shot as well and it

didn't bother him. It was almost as if he thrived on the stick he was getting. The experience he got in the Championship was invaluable. He came back to us as a confident lad – and stronger. He's always had a terrific attitude to work. There's a perception of how he is; brash and loud. But he's the quietest-spoken lad.

Stevie May, Striker, 22
I had made some appearances for Saints before, scored my first goal for the club in 2009, and then had my loan spells at Alloa and Hamilton. But it was always in my head that I had to prove myself, not just to the manager but the fans, and thankfully I managed to do that relatively quickly.

Callum Davidson
Pre-season was pretty good. The boys were good to be fair, probably could have given me a harder time than they did! I knew we had good, experienced players, so you know you probably need to coach the younger ones more. You make sure the older ones are fit and ready to play on a match day and are organised – and they were. Brian Easton came in, as did Gary McDonald, Gary Miller and David Wotherspoon – there were a few. With our ideas and training methods, we try and make it enjoyable for them. I look back on my experiences as a player and try to use them.

Steven Anderson, Defender, 29
The manager hasn't changed much, to be honest. The boys have the same mentality, and he just added a few new faces that summer. Stevie May came onto the scene as well, scoring goals.

18 July 2013: Newsflash...
'St Johnstone pulled off a shock win in their Europa League second qualifying round first leg match in Norway, as defender Frazer Wright's first-half goal stunned Rosenborg' (*The Scotsman*)

Tommy Wright

I remember I went over to watch Rosenborg against Crusaders and I had a team in my head. Rosenborg played quite a high line and I was thinking Stevie May would be brilliant to run in behind. Of course, didn't he bloody well get injured before the first game away! But we did ever so well away from home to win 1-0. It was a great first game in charge.

Steven Anderson

There was no pressure on us going into the Rosenborg game; they were the favourites – big budget, big team.

David Wotherspoon, Midfielder, 25

I wasn't part of the team the season before we got into Europe. I came in from Hibs, and then I'm starting my first game in Europe for my hometown team, the team I supported as a boy. It was actually nice, because it didn't feel like there was a lot of pressure. We were going in as underdogs, with nothing to lose, so we just enjoyed it, basically. 'Midge' (Chris Millar) was doing his video work at the same time, which was actually quite funny, so everyone was just enjoying it and having a good time. To get the result, we couldn't believe it.

Chris Millar, Midfielder, 32

I had made plans to start a journalism degree, so having read up on it I knew I had to do different things. I thought a video diary on our progress at the start of the season was a good idea. Brian Easton had just signed and was travelling up with me on one of his first days. I put my iPhone on, filming him on the way up, asking questions and filming training, just trying to document things.

Going to Rosenborg and winning turned out to be one of the greatest results in the club's history. It was good doing the video – the more it went on the more receptive the boys were and the gaffer was really good allowing me access. It just went really well and the boys enjoyed it. Looking back in 10 or 15 years, or whatever, there are some good memories on the video.

Gary McDonald, Midfielder, 33

It was a great start to the season. Rosenborg away was my first game for the club after signing in the summer, as it was for people like David. You couldn't have asked for a bigger stage, a better first game really, and we went from there.

Chris Millar

Being over there, for the players, the fans, everyone, was just great to be involved in that type of tie. They had been to the quarter-finals of the Champions League in the late 1990s so nobody really gave us a chance. But we thought on any given day you can win. We were relaxed and just looked forward to it. Before the game, watching them warm up, they just seemed to think all they had to do was turn up. They were laughing and joking and you just had a wee sense that they were maybe taking us a little bit lightly in terms of their body language. Their crowd was down, it wasn't a big crowd, and we thought if we could start really well we could cause them problems. Winning 1-0 was a famous victory for us. It started the season brilliantly and we were on a high.

Frazer Wright

I was delighted to score the winner over there and it gave us a belief in the camp so early in the season.

Callum Davidson

Winning at Rosenborg was a great experience. I remember sitting after about 70 minutes and Tommy was asking me who was picking up who at corners. I said 'I don't know'. He said 'well you've got the sheet'. I didn't realise I had to take all the set pieces out with me! He was going mental! That was kind of my first experience of being assistant manager, what I got wrong!

Gary McDonald

Nobody fancied us, but after we won over there, everybody expected us to then get through which perhaps reversed it a wee bit and put pressure on the home game.

26 July 2013: Newflash...
'Super Saints in dreamland as Wright's heroes slay Norwegians! Two games after being appointed St Johnstone manager, the genial Northern Irishman has assumed legendary status.' (*Mail Online*)

Tommy Wright

The same team was picked for the Perth game, but Chris Millar got injured. I had other options, so I was thinking 'do I keep the same team, or do I play Steven MacLean deeper and play Stevie May up top, which is more attacking with a 1-0 lead from the first leg?' Callum, Alex and myself were discussing it and Callum said 'remember what you said about Crusaders when you first saw Rosenborg?' so we went with May. We had another option that night, I think we could have just swapped a midfielder, but we didn't, as we dropped 'Macca' deeper and played Stevie up.

Steven MacLean, Striker, 32

Stevie played through the middle, and I dropped back towards midfield. Stevie had been brilliant in training, but after the great win in Rosenborg I don't think the gaffer would have changed the team until Millar pulled up in training. I remember the gaffer phoning me, saying 'you will need to play a little bit deeper as I'm going to play Stevie, he has been on fire.' From then, 'Mayso' never looked back. It was a great decision by the manager.

Tommy Wright

May might not have played that night – and if he hadn't you never know how everything would have panned out! That's the thing about sport, anything can happen, sometimes you get that wee bit of luck I suppose. You have decisions to make and sometimes they can turn out to be right. His goal against Rosenborg raised him to a level and we knew then that if he played most of the season, we were quite confident, basically, that he'd easily get into double figures.

Stevie May

It was fortunate getting my chance against Rosenborg, that's football. Getting that chance, I had to make the most of it and thankfully it went to plan. You need that little bit of luck, but if I hadn't played then it would only have been a matter of time before I got my chance. The gaffer had made that clear as well. It was a big step up for me, having been out on loan, but it was a great experience to play in the European game and score for the 1-1 draw at home that took us through (2-1 on aggregate).

Chris Millar

You can credit me for Stevie getting his chance! Seriously, I'm sure he would have broken through that season anyway but it just shows you how some things work out. Obviously, I had played in the first game, and in training a couple of days before the second leg I picked up a wee groin strain. Stevie got the nod and went in and scored the goal that took us into the next round. That goal just catapulted him from there – he never looked back, had a fantastic season and scored a lot of goals for us. It's just funny how things work out in football sometimes. I'm not saying it was fate, but it looks a wee bit as if it was meant to be. You look at the cup final as well, with May 17, it was like it was written that way to happen. Football sometimes works that way.

Stevie May

I got the No 17 shirt at the start of the season. If I remember rightly, I was meant to be getting the No 14 but we got a loan player back in, Gwion Edwards. He got re-signed on loan, so he got his No 14 back and then I got moved up to 17. I didn't request it, it was just given to me. It's funny the way it worked out, I know.

Steven MacLean

To be honest, I think it was just a matter of time before 'Mayso' got in and played because he was doing so well and looked so sharp in training. In bounce games or friendlies, he looked good. That day against Rosenborg, it was a typical Stevie goal. A nothing ball over the top and he made the most of it, nipped in front of the keeper to score, and from then on he never looked back.

Tommy Wright

Off the cuff, it wasn't really meant as a target, I said to May 'if you play a full season you will get 20 goals'. I didn't expect him to get 27, but he did.

Gary McDonald

We lost an early goal that night against Rosenborg which levelled it all out, but we did well to come back from that. It was a brilliant result for the club so early in the season.

Alan Mannus, Goalkeeper, 32

The Rosenborg game got us off to a good start, gave us that momentum and we went on from there. Rosenborg are such a big club and all the supporters who were at the second leg knew how big a game that was for us to get through. You could see what it meant to us after the game and how disappointed Rosenborg were after getting put out by St Johnstone. Most of them just went off the pitch, I think, they didn't even shake our hands, which showed the way they felt about it. But not only did we get a good result against Rosenborg, I thought we played very well in the two games and that set us up for the season.

Tommy Wright

Afterwards, you think 'I've got a goalscorer who can help win you a game and I've also got that organisation, discipline and desire not to get beaten'. That desire is an unbelievable quality to have, and people who want to defend. Getting David Wotherspoon in was key. What happened to David at Hibs should never happen to anybody. He played seven Scottish Cup ties for Hibs, wasn't on the losing side, and missed two finals (2012 & 2013) – never got stripped.

David Wotherspoon

The fans turned up for the Rosenborg tie as well, which was great to see. It was a brilliant night.

Alan Mannus

Playing in ties like Rosenborg was superb. I was playing in Northern Ireland up until the age of 27, which is a part-time league. I was at Linfield for 11 years from when I was 16, training two nights a week really. From there I went to Dublin and Shamrock Rovers, who play in the League of Ireland. I was sort of in between part-time and full-time. Coming here, I knew that, basically, Peter Enckelman was going to be playing and I had to just wait for my opportunity if I was going to get one. I was prepared to do that, as I had been trying to get over to England or Scotland since I was a teenager really to play full-time football. It took a good six months or so until I got a chance to play and then things just went really well for me, and the club.

Nigel Hasselbaink, Forward, 24

There was big confidence at the club because we had done well in the Europa League.

Tommy Wright

I think going into the European campaign the seeds of potential success started with me thinking, 'if we play like this in one off games, we can beat anybody, even the top teams, like if we did meet a Celtic.' The European performances proved that we were difficult to beat, how we were set up and organised, and then with the emergence of Stevie May to give you that spark, we had almost the perfect ingredients to be a really good cup side.

Steven Anderson

The manager did say that he felt we were a cup team, could go on a cup run and win something. But we've had so many semi-finals that it was frustrating.

Brian Easton

I had just signed, and was buzzing having seen the way they played away to Rosenborg. I thought we could do really well in the season, but I wasn't thinking about the Scottish Cup final.

Steven Anderson

I know we did well against Rosenborg (and then lost on penalties in the next round against FC Minsk), but you don't think about what you can achieve against other teams going forward. Every single game is the same, you go to win it. We had had cup runs before and I thought we had that togetherness as a team and as a squad to go and win something. I knew we did, and we showed that.

2

LIONS TAMED

I am obsessed.
I will follow you from Muirton to Timbuktu,
At McDiarmid, I'll back the boys in blue.

'Fair Maid'
The Shrugs

30 November 2013, McDiarmid Park
Scottish Cup Fourth Round: St Johnstone 2, Livingston 0

Mannus; Mackay, Jahic, Scobbie, Easton; Davidson (Caddis), Millar, McDonald, Hasselbaink (Fallon), Wotherspoon; May.
Goals: May 24, Jahic 62.

AFTER THE CLUB'S European adventure, domestic duties began promisingly for Saints with a three-game unbeaten league run, including an opening day success against Hearts and a thumping 4-0 win over Ross County. The following week it was Saints on the end of the same scoreline as Dundee United eased to victory at Tannadice. Nobody knew at the time how important that setback was and the valuable lessons learned. Impressive triumphs over Hamilton and Inverness were achieved, while a four-game winning run from the end of October was highlighted by a controversial last-gasp 1-0 League Cup quarter-final success at Morton to book a last-four meeting with Aberdeen at Tynecastle. Stevie May had quickly become a fans' favourite, scoring 11 goals in 19 appearances, to attract interest from clubs *south of the border. Meantime, winger Lee Croft returned to Saints to sign on, having previously played on loan, but striker Steven MacLean was back on the sidelines with another knee injury. With dreams still alive in the League Cup, another campaign began in earnest...*

Dave Mackay, Defender & Captain, 35

Going into another cup campaign, sometimes it's hard when you have come so close to finals so many times. Over my career, I've had six semi-finals losses. They are hard to take, but it just gives you more motivation to try and go that step further and get to a final. I had already been to a final with Dundee (Scottish Cup, 2003), but you just want to win a competition. Certainly, at my age, the older you get the more you feel as though it's never going to happen, so you're desperate to lift a trophy and get a medal to your name.

Tommy Wright

The club had cup pedigree, I knew that. But it was 2011 when they had last had a good cup run, losing 3-0 to Motherwell in the Scottish Cup semi-final at Hampden, so we all wanted to push on and try again.

Callum Davidson

It is tough being in the dugout after you've finished playing, but our start to the season in Europe and in the league was really good which made it easier. My wife, Lorna, will tell you that when we get beaten it's even worse now when I go home at night. If we get beaten on a Saturday, she knows straight away when I walk in the door, without knowing the result.

23 October 2013: Newsflash...
'St Johnstone have completed the signing of Bosnian international defender Sanel Jahic on a short-term deal until the New Year. The 31-year-old has spent the past

week training in Perth and will provide cover for the injured Steven Anderson and the suspended Frazer Wright.' (*Sky Sports online*)

Tommy Wright
Things were going well and I'm sure we were about sixth in the table when we went and watched Livingston. We were expected to win against Livi, but I knew they were a very good footballing side and I knew they would cause us problems.

David Wotherspoon
It's always a tough game when you play against teams that are not in the same league as you. I felt there was always pressure on us to go through.

Tommy Wright
The problem we had at that time was that we were short of centre backs, so I was fortunate enough to pick up Sanel Jahic. We got him for very little, hundreds of pounds. It was one of those short-term signings. I think we were down to four defenders at that time. Sanel had 20 caps for Bosnia and he came in and did a job for us, which we needed.

Steven MacLean
Sanel did well for us, he was a good lad. I remember he came in on trial and he was a big centre-back, as hard as nails. I remember in training I kicked lumps out of him one day, just booted him all over... and then the gaffer ended up signing him! The boys were having a laugh saying 'he's going to turn up and kill you.'

Steven Anderson
Sanel was a nice guy, a decent player and had played at a good standard with his national team.

Sanel Jahic, Defender, 33

I was very satisfied to play for St Johnstone. I was a free player, I came to St Johnstone and this time helped me a lot. The team had some problems in defence and I was delighted to play, they gave me a chance to help the team and to prove myself. It was a good moment for me. My time there helped me get to a bigger club. I was very happy there. I was satisfied with the ambition of the club, of the atmosphere in the club and I was very happy to play.

Dave Mackay

When you play a lower league team, it's always important to get the first goal. You certainly don't want to go behind as they have something to hang on to, and they can sit in as you try to break them down. You are likely then to be hit on the break. It's always really important to get the first goal, which we've been really good at over the years in the cup competitions against lower league teams. You always fancy your chances if you go a goal ahead, which we did thankfully.

Stevie May

It was a home tie against a lower league side and we've proven over the last few years that we can take care of them and manage to get results. It shows the type of player we have at the club, very professional and they get the job done. Livi had a few chances, but we won the game. I scored the first goal, a shot from just outside the box, and it was Sanel who got the second from close in (from a corner from David Wotherspoon).

Murray Davidson, Midfielder, 27

Games like that one against my old club Livingston – at home to lower league teams – are where you have to be focused, knowing if you play to your best you should go through. Dave Mackay and I signed from Livi and we had beaten them before in a

League Cup tie, back in 2011. We weren't at our best on the day to win 2-0 in the Scottish Cup, but we were professional and we progressed. My claim to fame is setting up 'Mayso' for the first goal. That was my part in the Scottish Cup run!

Sanel Jahic
It was my first game and it was great to score a goal. It wasn't very easy, but cup games are always difficult to win. It was a hard game for us, but we won. I scored and I was very happy.

Tam Scobbie, Defender, 27
'Sanny' had come in, so we had to chop and change the back four a little. They put us under quite a bit of pressure, but we've good players in the squad and I thought we dealt with it well. The game just set us up for an unbelievable run in the cup.

David Wotherspoon
The boys dealt with it well. They had threats from a couple of players that are now down south, obviously the pick of the bunch. We were always threatening to score and once we did we eased into the game and it took the pressure off us.

Brian Easton
I remember it being quite scrappy, but thinking 'we're not going to get beaten, if we get a goal we'll get through here.' When you do get a tie like that at home, it's all about the right attitude and we showed it, not just against Livi but against other lower league teams that season.

Gary McDonald
It wasn't a game where I felt we were under any real pressure. I thought we were quite comfortable. I don't remember them having any clear-cut chances. It's about getting the first goal in those games. Once you do that, you can relax a bit more.

Alan Mannus

With it being a cup game, anything can happen. We were probably expected to win, being the league above them. But, credit to them, I thought they played excellently and played some really good football. I remember having to make two or three saves and being busy enough. Once we got the second goal, we were comfortable after that. It was good to get the result, get into the next round and the clean sheet was a nice bonus for us as well.

Tam Scobbie

Livingston played really well and put us under a bit of pressure. It was one of those games, playing against lower league opposition, it could have been a banana skin, but we were very professional the way we went about it and the result kicked us on. The manager had spoken even before the game about how he wanted a cup run. He believed that with the players we had, if we got a little bit of luck and put in some good performances, we could go all the way – and that was proved come the end of the season.

Nigel Hasselbaink

Livingston was a difficult game for us, but we got through it and that was the main thing.

Liam Caddis, Midfielder, 21

I came on as a sub against Livingston, before soon going out on loan to Alloa. It was great to be involved in the cup campaign.

Tommy Wright

It wasn't the prettiest of games, but we got through it. That's all you can do, get through, get in the hat and look for the draw. It brought up Forfar, away.

Sanel Jahic

When I signed for St Johnstone, the target was to be as high as possible in the league and to try to go as far as possible in the cups. I knew they were a good Scottish club with a good team in a tough league. It was a nice time for me there and I was very happy to be a part of the team that started the cup run.

Tommy Wright
I was already enjoying the job, being in charge. I've worked with some big names, like Glenn Roeder, Kevin Keegan and Joe Royle, but first and foremost you are what you are. You have to be yourself. You are subconsciously influenced by them, but you're not going 'Billy Bingham used to do this with Northern Ireland and so on.' I just think all your experiences make you what you are.

I'd like to think I'm a wee bit of all my past managers, but I think my biggest strength is probably my man-management skills. I think I manage players well. I'm always honest with them, not like Ossie Ardiles...! I remember Ossie was one of my bosses at Newcastle, but he wasn't picking me. He was the type of manager who stuck by his first XI, which was great, if you were one of the XI. Pavel Srnicek was the first-choice goalkeeper. Eventually Pav got injured and I came in. We lost 1-0 at Middlesbrough but I played really well. Ossie said he wanted to give me a new contract. I said 'Okay, but I want you to tell me why you haven't been giving me a game'. He said he'd seen me playing for Northern Ireland a while back and he wasn't impressed. 'I'd had a poor match,' he said. He told me the game, the date, the venue, but he'd got the wrong guy. I said 'Ossie, that was Allen McKnight, not me.' He said, 'Really?' Ossie was priceless, so laid-back. No structure. Just turn up and play, play, play.

I'm always honest with my players, I'm up front. I'll tell them why they're not in the team. I'll praise them, and I'll rollock them. If I rollock them, it's forgotten about, I move on, I don't hold things. So what they get is basically what they see and I think that's important. I'm very inclusive in terms of my staff, I have them all muck in and question me, but they know at the end of the day the final decision is mine. I wouldn't like to think I'm any of the managers that I worked under, but I'd like to think they've all probably influenced me.

3

FLOURISH AT FORFAR

I'll follow the Saints through the glory and the strife,
Our love is unrestricted.

'Fair Maid'
The Shrugs

8 February 2014, Station Park
Scottish Cup Fifth Round: Forfar 0, St Johnstone 4

Banks; Mackay, Wright, Anderson, Easton; Croft, Cregg, McDonald
(Brown), Wotherspoon (Dunne); O'Halloran, May (Iwelumo).
Goals: May 27, Wright 42, O'Halloran 64, Dunne 80.

IF 2013 HAD ended in style for Saints with a 3-0 win over
Dundee United, the New Year soon began on a low note with
back-to-back defeats to Motherwell and Ross County. There
was further disappointment when midfielder Murray Davidson
was ruled out for the rest of the season due to knee surgery after
landing awkwardly in a 3-3 draw with Hearts at McDiarmid
Park. However, sandwiched in between were league wins over
St Mirren and Partick, while the squad was bolstered with
the arrivals of Michael O'Halloran, Chris Iwelumo and James
Dunne. Sadly, the League Cup semi-final against Aberdeen
proved a disappointing day, but the chance to atone in another
cup competition came at Station Park just a week later...

Tommy Wright

We were obviously all hurting after the Aberdeen result, losing 4-0. I knew that defeat was another sort of scar on the likes of Anderson, Mackay and Millar who had probably played in most of the semi-finals the club had recently been in.

For people like Wright and MacLean, who missed that semi-final due to his knee injury, it was the same. We had a squad of good pros who had decent careers but hadn't really won anything, and you get so close that it hurts. The Aberdeen defeat hurt. The 4-0 scoreline hurt.

Chris Millar

Personally, I had been to a few semi-finals with St Johnstone and never quite made that final, so it was something I wanted to achieve in my career. I remember we lost 2-0 to Rangers in the League Cup semi-final in 2010 on a wintry night. I thought we did enough to win that game, but we missed chances and Rangers were two ahead at half-time. I missed the 3-0 defeat to Motherwell in the Scottish Cup semi-final the following season due to a groin injury after failing a fitness test the morning of the game. They started brilliantly and deservedly went through to the final, but those are memories you want to put right.

The same could be said of the League Cup semi-final against Aberdeen. I thought we were excellent at times, but they were clinical. 4-0 sounds like a heavy defeat, but at 1-0 Lee Croft had a great chance and then mistakes ended up costing us. We were caught with sucker punch counter attacks.

I've won the First Division with Saints, and won the Second and Third with Morton, so the next thing for me, setting targets, was always to win a cup. I believed we had a great chance and the draw was kind to us in the earlier rounds of the Scottish Cup. We saw them as favourable draws and always believed we could win them.

Lee Croft, Midfielder, 29

Losing to Aberdeen spurred us on, as we wanted to then do well in another competition, make sure we went further than in the League Cup.

David Wotherspoon

It was a disappointing day against Aberdeen. I don't think the scoreline projected how well we played. I thought we did well in the first half and just conceded silly goals on counter attacks, especially in the second half, when we were chasing the game which left us open.

Gary McDonald

It was Aberdeen's day that day, I think. They got the breaks, which you need in semi-finals. It was probably one of the most disappointing days of my career and the next game really couldn't have come quickly enough. It was the best thing for us, a cup competition again.

Alan Mannus

I missed a few matches, including the Aberdeen and Forfar cup ties, after fracturing a bone in my thumb in training at the end of January. It was out of nothing, it was just the way the ball caught me on my thumb. You tend to hurt your fingers and your thumbs every few weeks, anyway. You sort of stave them. You see a lot of keepers tape their fingers and their thumbs up from injuries over the years. I just thought I had staved it really, just a bit of a sprain and kept on training. I didn't think it was broken at the time, then later back at home it was swelling up and getting quite painful.

We actually had a game the next night against Dundee United, but I was suspended for that anyway. It was called off because of the weather, so I called the physio and told him about the thumb and he wanted to have a look at it. I went up, met him, he said 'let's get it X-rayed' and it came back fractured, which was a bit of a surprise. The doctor at the hospital said it was probably going to be eight weeks before I could look to play again. I knew then I was going to miss a few games, which is not the best feeling when you get news like that, but I guess you go through it when you are a footballer.

Steve Banks, Goalkeeper, 43
With Alan injured, there was a spell of three games when I was in as cover. So it was nice to actually do something towards winning the cup because, for my previous two medals (Hearts and Dundee United), I was lucky enough to be involved on the bench, but didn't get a minute on the pitch.

At least I can say I contributed to this one! I was with Hearts in 2006 against Gretna and, four years later, I won another medal with Dundee United in the final against Ross County.

The reason I came to Scotland in the first place was because George Burley was manager at Hearts and Malcolm Webster was his goalkeeping coach assistant. It was a no-brainer to come up. They had big name players and a huge fan base. They were looking for someone to understudy Craig Gordon, who was in the Scotland squad. They wanted someone coming to the tail end of their playing career who would be happy to sit on the bench but be ready to do a job when required. That is still the case here with St Johnstone. It is a special niche. You could get a younger lad who has never been tried out, or you can go for a player with 15 or 20 years in the game.

Tommy Wright
We went to Forfar missing suspended Tam Scobbie and the injured trio of Murray Davidson, Alan Mannus and Steven MacLean, but we had managed to bring some lads in.

Chris Iwelumo, Striker, 36
I got the chance to come back to Scotland after 16 years, having left St Mirren when I was 19-years-old. Tommy Wright gave me that opportunity and, to be fair, I came into a squad where the confidence was there. I sensed early on they were capable of doing something. Everyone was on the same page in training and going into the games with a great attitude.

Dave Mackay
It was always going to be a tricky tie at Forfar, a League One side, the week after we had lost the semi-final to Aberdeen. The place was on a bit of a downer at the time – the fans, the players, everybody – and then we had another cup competition straight after it, so it was potentially a tricky one for us.

Tommy Wright
I didn't believe the performance was as bad as the scoreline looked in the Aberdeen semi-final, and we tried to get the positives out of it. The important thing was to bounce back and the one thing about the group of players, since I've been here, is that they've always bounced back from setbacks, they get through things – and that's what we did.

Callum Davidson
We got the Aberdeen semi-final defeat out of our system, going to compete in a different cup competition.

Tommy Wright
Again, I had watched Forfar, our scout Ewan Peacock had watched them, and we knew it was a game that was going to cause us difficulty. We knew the artificial pitch could be a bit of a leveller, but I always believe that when you are playing a team that you should beat on paper, it's all about attitude and preparation. So we prepared as if we were going to play the champions. We told

them what the dressing room was going to be like, we told them to go there, not to moan about anything, just get on with it, do our jobs and get out. Basically, we did that.

Steven Anderson

It was a potential banana skin up there, playing on the astroturf as well. It's not an easy place to go, the changing rooms and so on, but the boys showed their mentality to go there and comfortably beat them.

Patrick Cregg, Midfielder, 29

I knew we had a good squad and team – whatever side was put out – that could beat any team in the country on any given day. I wasn't thinking we were going to win the cup that season, but you always think you have a chance. I got to the Scottish Cup final with Falkirk (losing to Rangers in 2009) and, if you get a little bit of luck along the way, it's only four or five games to get to a cup final. It's a great chance every season to aim to reach one.

Stevie May

It could have been a tough one at Forfar, but it was always about getting that first goal – the longer we went on without getting it the tougher it would be. But, thankfully, it came in the first half when I hooked in from close range and the boys played well on the astroturf. It was after the Aberdeen semi-final defeat which was a tough day, but I think it helped us in the long run. We didn't want that to happen again. It happens in football, you learn from where you went wrong and get the experience from that.

Dave Mackay

I'd be lying if I said I wasn't surprised at how well Stevie May did for the whole season. He is a good player – he had scored goals on loan at Alloa and Hamilton, so he was obviously a natural goalscorer. To have the same sort of campaign in his first season in the top flight, a lot of the time playing up front on his own due to 'Macca' being injured, it was incredible the amount of goals he scored. Unfortunately for us, we ended up losing him due to his goals, but he made a huge impact and one you didn't quite see happening so quickly.

Patrick Cregg
I remember one day in the dressing room when May was out on loan at Hamilton. I just remember saying to the boys 'he will be a Scottish internationalist'. I was proved right! Hopefully if I become a coach or a manager, I've got a good eye for a player.

Alex Cleland
We always knew Stevie was a really good player and it was just a matter of managing Stevie, coaching him and adding little things to his game – because he was a natural goal scorer from an early age. I worked with him from the age of 17 and it was great to see him develop. When he first came in he was working with the youth coaches, before we got him full-time with the Under-19s. He then took the next step by going out on loan and scoring goals for·Alloa and Hamilton, coming back a better all-round player. Stevie just needed to be developed – and he has developed really well. We were absolutely delighted with the impact he made, scoring goals very quickly. Latterly, the chairman was obviously delighted we could get money for a player who had come through our youth system – that is really rewarding for everyone at the club.

Tommy Wright
It was a 3pm kick-off at Forfar and we had heard that Celtic had been knocked out at home to Aberdeen at lunchtime. We were professional, ruthless and got first half goals from Stevie and Frazer.

Frazer Wright

I scored a header from about a yard, just my distance! The longer it goes 0-0 in those games, your opponents can get more belief and you can start getting a bit nervous.

David Wotherspoon

They have their astroturf and you're not used to it. I don't think we dominated but I felt comfortable.

Gary McDonald

I felt comfortable, the first goal was important. The astro was actually a good leveller for us, because when you go away from home against these teams and you get a dodgy pitch, it helps them. On the astro, I thought we passed it fairly well.

Chris Millar

I remember being on the bench at Forfar. The gaffer said he was going to make some changes in the earlier rounds. Obviously, you want to play, but you understand the nature of the game and squad rotation. The gaffer calls the shots – it is part and parcel of football, so you just have to accept it. But you want to play in every round because a cup is always something I felt we could win. We are probably never going to win the league, so finishing in the top six is always our aim at the start of season, as well as trying to win a cup. Going back to playing under Derek McInnes, he always said that, for a club like St Johnstone, it should be their aim to try and win a cup.

Steve Banks

It was a tricky tie for us at Forfar, playing on their artificial surface on a horrible day. They fancied their chances of an upset. I remember just getting a touch to a 30-yard shot (from Odmar Faeroe) to push it onto the crossbar. It was 2-0 at the time so it was important.

Alan Mannus

Steve made an unbelievable save, although I don't think people realised he got a touch on the ball. It was maybe just the angle where I was standing that I could see that he touched it onto the bar. It was the type of thing he does every day in training. When he has played games, he has kept clean sheets and done well.

Tommy Wright

James Dunne had come in by this time, because Murray Davidson suffered that horrific injury against Hearts. We were picking up injuries but, fair play to the chairman, he backed us and brought people in to replace them. James then proved to be a key player the rest of the season. Michael O'Halloran came in as well and scored at Forfar.

James Dunne, Midfielder, 25

It was a bit unfortunate for Murray to pick up that injury, but it opened the door for me really. I wasn't playing at Stevenage, I was sitting in the stands there, so I needed to get out on loan to play a bit of football. I ended up coming to St Johnstone and it turned out alright, to be fair! I had a couple of offers, but St Johnstone were still in the hunt for two cups, so I chose to go to them. I came the week of the Aberdeen League Cup semi-final – the game was on the Saturday – so it wasn't really ideal for me, especially having not played for a while. I wasn't expecting to go straight in anyway.

Michael O'Halloran, Forward, 24

It was my first start at Forfar and I scored. After the Aberdeen semi-final defeat, we had a lot of determination to go again. When I first arrived, I thought we had a great set of lads and all the staff around the club work so hard as well. When you come to a new club you want to make an impression and it was a great game to do that.

Gary McDonald

Michael came in on his first start and scored, with Dunne scoring too. Throughout the season you need guys like that to come in and do well, you need your full squad. I don't think that was highlighted any more clearly than during that game.

James Dunne

I came on as sub with about 20 minutes to go, and scored a goal as well, which was even better on my debut. It wasn't too bad a strike, a left foot volley, and we were into the quarter-finals.

Frazer Wright

Dunne made a real impact when he came here, and Michael as well, to be fair.

Scott Brown, Midfielder, 20

I got about 10 minutes against Forfar when we were 4-0 up at the time. It was good to get on and play a part in the cup run.

Steve Banks

It was nice to bounce back with a decent performance and a good win. I think my experience of the 4-0 defeat to Aberdeen helped that day, no question. That game was the very reason I'm doing what I'm doing. If it had been a young boy in goal that day against Aberdeen it could have ruined his career. We had gone into it with high hopes of reaching a final. I have been in those predicaments before and I'm old enough and ugly enough to handle it. I knew I had to get on with it.

Brian Easton

I remember (Forfar manager) Dick Campbell in the papers afterwards, he said he didn't realise how good a side St Johnstone was, because we went up there and treated it like any other Premiership game. We did play well.

Nigel Hasselbaink

In the cup you never know what can happen, no matter who you are playing, a big team or a smaller team.

Dave Mackay

It was good to actually get through that tie pretty comfortably in the end. Dunne scored a good goal in the second half. We felt we had a great chance to go to the final of the League Cup and the fans were obviously thinking 'it's another defeat, we're never going to get over that hurdle'. So to make sure we got through the Forfar tie was hugely important for us.

Stevie May

It's always good to score goals, the fans certainly like players who score. It was becoming a good season, we were sitting OK in the league but we still had that disappointment from the Aberdeen semi-final defeat and we were looking to put that right. It would have been nice to have gone further in the League Cup, but the Scottish Cup is the big one, probably the one you want to win just that little bit more.

Patrick Cregg

I lived together with 'Mayso' for six months in Perth the previous season. That cup-winning season he was probably my best friend on the team, along with Lee Croft, Nigel Hasselbaink, who lived near us as well, and the lads who signed in January, big Chris Iwelumo and James Dunne. We all went to training together, and were all good friends.

Chris Iwelumo

I had a fantastic car school. There was me, 'Mayso', Dunne, Croft, Tim Clancy, 'Padge' Cregg and Nigel. That was the car school. We were the Perth boys driving to Stirling for training. We were together a lot, in hotels, travelling to training, going for lunch afterwards, having dinner together in the evening some nights. It was a good group.

Stevie May
Croft, 'Padge' and myself took them under our wing, we had a little car school, about seven of us always travelling to training. It was nice to have the close group as it was good for team spirit.

Chris Iwelumo
My whole time at St Johnstone was a fantastic experience. They had a great squad, great players and everything just clicked for them. It was so well organised, from even above the gaffer, people like (football administrator) Paul Smith behind the scenes, the chairman and the owner. It's a family club. I know a lot of clubs don't like being called that, but everything was just right. The boys were always on it in training, it was just a great place to be and I really enjoyed my time there. Every single day it was a great place to be and that's obviously why they achieved such great things that season.

Tommy Wright
It was a professional, good all-round performance at Forfar – job done and let's move onto the next one. You then start to look at the draw and have a wee think.

4

BREEZING INTO THE SEMIS

Will we go down in history,
For now it's a mystery.

'Fair Maid'
The Shrugs

8 March 2014, Stark's Park
Scottish Cup Quarter-Final: Raith Rovers 1, St Johnstone 3

Mannus; Miller, Mackay, Anderson, Easton; Croft (Millar), Dunne, McDonald; MacLean, Hasselbaink (Wotherspoon), May (O'Halloran). Goals: McDonald 4, Hasselbaink 49, Anderson 79.

NOT FOR THE first time in recent years, the Scottish Cup was wide open. Raith Rovers, Dumbarton, Albion Rovers and Rangers all remained in the competition, with St Johnstone, Aberdeen, Inverness Caledonian Thistle and Dundee United the last top-flight teams left standing. Saints had started to stutter and arrived at Stark's Park with just one win in their last four league matches. But with Stevie May still flourishing, scoring 21 goals in all competitions, and Steven MacLean back in the fold after his injury troubles, confidence was high going to Kirkcaldy...

Brian Easton
When the draw for the last eight came out, you're thinking 'there

is a chance of the semi-finals', but it was an away game and we couldn't turn up just thinking we would win.

Tommy Wright

In my head, already at this stage, I was thinking 'this could be our year'. It was probably the first time I thought about it. I'd made that one-liner to the chairman who had said 'you know you've got to win a cup in your first season' and I said 'yeah, I will'. It was a joke, but that came back into my thinking when we got to Raith.

Steven Anderson

We couldn't think too far ahead. It was a good draw, but it was all about tunnel vision. Focus on the tie and get through it, no matter how you do it.

Tommy Wright

The good thing about playing Raith was the result they achieved against Hibs (winning 3-2 at Easter Road in the previous round). I used that. I said 'look, this is what will happen to us if we're not at our best.' I said 'don't get carried away, don't be thinking we're in the semi-finals, you've a job to do'.

Alan Mannus

I had come back from injury a bit earlier than expected for the league games prior to the quarter-final because I was basically able to strap up my thumb with a metal bar. It was about the length of the thumb, about seven centimetres. It was a wee strip of metal that taped on to my thumb to hold it in place and hopefully stop such an injury from happening again. I felt that I could start training again ahead of schedule and our physio was OK with me doing that. My first game back was against Celtic in mid-February and I just wore that metal bar on my thumb for the rest of the season. It was a bit annoying, but it was necessary really.

Steven MacLean

I had managed to come back early, too, after my knee injury. I damaged my cruciate ligament when I was only 16 so I knew the day would come that I would get problems with my knee as I got older in my career. I've had a bit of a nightmare at St Johnstone with injuries and when I had the micro fracture during the 2013-14 season, the surgeon wasn't sure if he was going to be able to do anything. I thought my career could have been over. I had a few dark days and nights wondering if he was going to be able to fix it. Luckily enough, he was able to do the micro fracture operation and sort the knee.

When he fixed it, I was hopeful I was going to make the League Cup semi-final against Aberdeen but he didn't want me coming back as quickly as that. I was gutted. I was just hoping the boys were going to stay in the Scottish Cup and I could get another crack at it. I managed to come back early for the Motherwell game in late February when the gaffer threw me in and I scored two goals. Then we played Aberdeen away and I got sent off. I thought I might miss the Raith cup game, which was the next match, but because I was sent off in the league I missed a league game.

Nigel Hasselbaink

Everyone was pleased with the draw, getting Raith Rovers. It was a game we could win.

James Dunne

A game like that can go either way, really. You know what the Scottish Cup is like. It was good to score early on, as I remember on the day the wind was really bad. Every time Alan, our goalkeeper, kicked a ball it literally just hung up in the air and our centre-halves had to come and challenge for it.

Alan Mannus

It was a lunchtime kick-off and it was very, very windy. In the first half we were against the wind so it made it even more difficult. The ball can come right back at you. As we were at Raith's ground, the ball was also different from what we had been using. You use the ball of the home team. If it was a Scottish Premiership team, you would use their ball and vice versa if it was a Championship team. So the ball was actually a wee bit different, it was a lot lighter.

David Wotherspoon
You are hoping for a good tie, but it wasn't the easiest as it was away from home and it's quite open at Stark's Park.

Steven Anderson
It was blowing a gale, the pitch wasn't the best and it's always a very hard place to go.

Steven MacLean
It was definitely a tricky game. Listen, when you get a lower league team in the quarter-finals you've got to be happy, although potentially it's a banana skin. We were confident going there. We took the lead very early on, when it dropped to Gary McDonald – it was a great finish.

Callum Davidson
I think it was a set piece we had worked on, Gary's goal. It was a wee chipped ball in and a wee knock down. It was a great finish.

Gary McDonald
Gary Miller played it in, a lofted ball that held up in the wind and it was 'Ando' who knocked it down. We had worked on that move, but on that type of day you're just trying to pick up the pieces off the second ball.

Gary Miller, Defender, 28
You're always working hard and waiting for your chance and I

got the chance against Raith at right-back. Dave Mackay moved into the centre as Frazer Wright was out, injured. Gary volleyed it right-footed, a great volley, into the bottom corner. It was after only four minutes so we were obviously delighted to get on our way early in the game.

Steven MacLean
Normally, when we go ahead in games, we don't normally get beaten. But, to be fair to Raith, they came into the game very well. It was really, really windy and they battered us for a while, scoring a wonder goal to equalise.

Dave Mackay
Joe Cardle scored an absolute screamer to level, which we really couldn't do much about. You are a bit nervy then.

Alan Mannus
They had a couple of decent chances in the first half and I obviously remember the goal – it was an unbelievable strike. The ball just flew. I dived and stretched as far as I could but it went in off the post. What can you do whenever you get a strike like that?

James Dunne
Gary scored early for us, which kind of quietened them down a bit. Then obviously they got the equaliser and I thought they probably should have had another one before half-time, but they missed their chances.

Gary McDonald
We had a couple of scary moments before half-time, which probably came at the right time for us, to be honest. But the gaffer had a few words at half-time and I think we came out the traps quite well in the second half.

Steven MacLean

We needed to get into half-time and reorganise, because the conditions were helping them more than us. I don't think we played that well and we could probably have been behind at half-time. I remember the gaffer came in and had a bit of a go at us. But we came out in the second half and were excellent.

Tommy Wright

There was nothing in the game at half-time and we needed a spark. Nigel provided it. It was a really good goal, a really good finish from him, and then we controlled the game.

Nigel Hasselbaink

It was a very tight game. They scored an unbelievable goal to make it 1-1, but we still believed in ourselves. Just after half-time, I had probably my best moment in the cup-winning run to put us ahead. It was a good feeling for me to score in the game as it was a very important goal. When I scored that goal, I felt great, not only me, but for everyone in the team. We were all thinking after that win at Raith that things could happen for us – this can be our year in the cup.

Callum Davidson

Nigel was quite lucky probably still to be on the pitch at that point! He wasn't having his greatest game. We were giving him some time after half-time – Nigel probably doesn't know that! But, in the end, it shows how things can change sometimes and how funny things are. We were thinking how could we change it and then Nigel produces his goal. It was a difficult game, but we came through it with a battling performance. We got more width in the team in the second half and started to cause them more problems.

Stevie May

It was a tough day, it was blowing a gale and the conditions were terrible. It was always going to be a tough one, perhaps won by the odd goal, and Nigel scored a great goal. It settled us and we managed to go on and win 3-1 in the end. I remember Cardle scored that world-class goal from 35 yards, but Nigel's goal was worthy of winning any game.

David Wotherspoon
Nigel scored a great goal at a great time for us. I think that just set us up for going on to win the match.

Gary McDonald
A toe poke from Nigel, wasn't it...?!

Nigel Hasselbaink
It was a toe poke finish, after I picked it up on the left and ran into the space between the defenders. I just hit it with my toe as hard as I could and the ball went in so well. It was a great feeling, to score at that stage in any game. After my goal, I think the game was a bit easier for us, but at 1-1 it was very difficult.

Gary Miller
We got a bit of a shock with their equaliser, but in the second half we picked up. There was a good belief in the squad that we could always be dangerous and we pushed forward and got the result in the end.

Brian Easton
When Nigel's goal went in, I was thinking 'we're alright here'. When we lost 'Macca' after the St Mirren game in mid-October for a wee while, I was thinking it was going to be a big loss for us. But other boys did step up, like wee 'Nige' who went up front and found his form. The first half had been edgy at Raith, but after he scored it was a lot more comfortable.

Chris Iwelumo

Of course, I could understand why I wasn't playing as much. 'Macca' was injured when I signed – I think that's why Tommy brought me in. Looking back, it's a little funny as the first game I was going to start was called off due to the rain, against Dundee United. It was written in the stars really, as 'Macca' came back to fitness that little bit earlier and in his first game back he scored those two goals against Motherwell. To be fair, he went on and performed unbelievably, scoring goals as well. With 'Mayso' scoring too, you couldn't really change things up front too much. There were also people like Nigel Hasselbaink, who was in and out of the team. He had more of a shout to play than me because he had been at the club for longer and had contributed a lot more. Nigel and guys like Gary Miller were on the bench with me, so I just enjoyed it, enjoyed being with that group of players.

Steven Anderson

We showed our resilience in the second half at Raith. The wind didn't help, we were kicking into it in the first half and the ball wasn't going far so we were under pressure. But we came out in the second half and played a lot better.

Alan Mannus

After the break we had the wind, which was a bit of an advantage for us, causing them problems. We got the second goal, although they had a couple of opportunities as well, like a free kick that bounced and I was pleased that I was able to hold onto it with the Raith lads all charging in at me. We got the third and it ended up being a great result for us against a team who did really well, battled, and gave us as many problems as any top flight team would.

Steven MacLean

Nigel scored a good individual goal, which he had in his locker.

He showed loads of power and pace, before 'Ando' popped up with a set play again and that made it comfortable to see the game out.

Steven Anderson
I scored a couple of goals around that time, so it was good to get the third at the front post against Raith to ease the pressure on us. Why did the goals start going in? Luck!

Lee Croft
We always felt that in the second half, with the wind, we could go and win it. It was my corner for 'Ando's' goal, a near post run... a great corner, we worked on that!

Frazer Wright
'Ando' has been making the same runs for 10 years – and they finally came off!

Gary McDonald
'Ando' did end up being on a good run of goals going into the cup final, so fair play to him.

James Dunne
Nigel changed the game really at Raith, scored a lovely goal, and then 'Ando' scored the third. We were into the semi-finals and in great spirits.

Gary Miller
It was a tough game, as it's always tough going to places like that. To go there and win and score three goals was great for us. I was fighting for my spot during the season, trying to get in the team and doing what I could. But we were doing so well, so it was always difficult. It was a good cup run for the team, but for me it was a bit in and out in terms of playing.

Tam Scobbie

I had picked up an injury against Inverness towards the end of February. It was disappointing, snapping ankle ligaments to finish my season. I had played quite a few games up to that point and we were playing really well, going into a lot of fixtures with confidence and we had a settled squad. It was just unfortunate for me, one of those things that happen in football and you just have to deal with it. I missed the League Cup semi-final at Tynecastle through suspension too, so I missed two semi-finals and a cup final that season. From a personal point of view, it wasn't a great end to the season not being involved, but for the other boys it was brilliant.

Dave Mackay

You look for a home tie in cup competitions, especially against teams from lower divisions, so the Raith tie was tricky. It was live on TV as well, which probably wasn't a great spectacle for the viewers given how the wind really affected the game. So to get through to the semi-finals we showed great character and belief as a team. We would have taken the Raith draw beforehand, but winning is easier said than done, as you've still got to go out and turn in a performance. We had three different scorers that day which showed the squad effort. Stevie May was a huge player for us that season, our most important player by a mile in terms of scoring goals and winning games, but it was definitely a team effort over the whole campaign.

Tommy Wright

Again, the players went out that day in horrible conditions and performed. We were looking at a second semi-final – in my first season with the players. That, in itself, was an incredible achievement.

19 March 2014: Newsflash...
'St Johnstone today announced that manager Tommy

Wright will have "a routine operation" after suffering stomach pains. Wright was taken to hospital earlier this week and was "detained overnight for observation". St Johnstone host Hibernian in the Scottish Premiership this weekend, with coaches Callum Davidson and Alex Cleland to prepare the team for a fixture that could decide which of the two sides secures a place in the top six this season.' (*BBC online*)

Tommy Wright

The stomach pains totally came out of the blue. It was a Sunday, I was taking Anne to the airport, and I had something to eat. On the way home from the airport I just took a pain in the middle of my chest. It wouldn't go away. It felt like I had wind. I was bringing wind up but nothing with it. The pain just wouldn't go away. I phoned the club doctor that night and he said 'see how you are overnight, take paracetamol, do the normal things, it might just be a bug that you've got.'

I went to bed, but I was up all night, sweating and the pain was just really bad. I got up and called the club doctor and he said you better go down to A&E. I phoned Roddy Grant (associate director) and he came and picked me up. The staff at Perth Royal Infirmary (PRI) checked me first of all for my heart, that was OK, but I still couldn't get rid of the pain. They gave me one morphine injection, two morphine injections, but still couldn't get rid of the pain. The first relief I had was later on that night when I threw up and all this bile stuff came up, so I was starting to think I'm going to get better now. That wasn't the case, and it wasn't until they put me on trapidol that I got pain relief. Then they found out what it was – it was my gallbladder.

I had absolutely no symptoms previously – it just came on the Sunday night. The doctors took me in, did all the scans, and said the gallbladder had to come out. They wanted to do keyhole, but it was that far gone that it was too dangerous so they had to slit me open and take it out. It was a close call, because they said that my gallbladder was close to basically disintegrating, just like breaking up. But they were great at PRI. So that was me in hospital and we had Hibs on the Saturday, needing a win for the top six. And me being me, Callum and Alex came up to the hospital and the three of us were organising training. I just couldn't stop – I needed something to keep me going. So we picked the team, Callum and Alex took it and we won 2-0 and we secured the top six again. It was then a slow process for me, building up my health again.

Callum Davidson

I was thrilled to oversee the victory against Hibs that clinched our top-six place with three games to spare. That was three times in a row making the top six, which is a big achievement for a club like St Johnstone. For me, it was different but Tommy was still phoning me every day! He couldn't speak that loud which was quite good! It was a good experience for me – we won both league games against Hibs and St Mirren – but really I was just holding the ropes until Tommy was back. He wasn't great.

Tommy Wright

I've got full trust in my backroom team and that's why I work with them. We've worked perfectly, along with the rest of the staff since I got the job. I know things are being well run, even when I'm not there. There isn't a 'them and us' with the players, but there is a line. Callum is very professional and has been a nice go-between with the players. We both still have a lot of banter with the players, but they do know there is a line you can't cross. I think, as a club, the staff and the players are all pretty much together; there is a great camaraderie between us all. Of course, I need support and Callum and Alex, in particular, are always there for me.

Steven Anderson

It was really annoying being a glorious failure by getting to semi-finals and losing. Honestly, it annoyed me, because this club has had many glorious failures when you think about it. I'd lost five semi-finals. You get frustrated and annoyed if you do lose, and we just wanted to put it right. I thought 'this is the time'.

Stevie May
I remember watching the draw with Croft and Dunne and I said 'I bet it's them again.' The draw didn't disappoint.

Gary McDonald
I thought it was going to happen (getting Aberdeen).

5

HISTORY BOYS

For you'll be my friend until the bitter end,
Perth St Johnstone, My Fair Maid.

'Fair Maid'
The Shrugs

13 April 2014, Ibrox Stadium
Scottish Cup Semi-Final: St Johnstone 2, Aberdeen 1

Mannus; Mackay, Anderson, Wright, Easton; Wotherspoon, Millar,
Dunne, O'Halloran (Cregg); MacLean, May.
Goals: May 61, 84.

FOR ABERDEEN, IT had already been a season of triumphant progress. Former Perth boss Derek McInnes guided his side to League Cup glory, the club's first trophy since 1995, and they were challenging strongly to finish second in the Premiership. Saints had failed to score in four games against the Dons during the season and were still licking their wounds from the League Cup semi-final exit to McInnes' men. Aberdeen brought a large support to Ibrox, sensing another final opportunity. However, Saints had suffered just one defeat in seven matches, sealed a top-six place for the third successive season and travelled determined to finally end their eight-game Scottish Cup semi-final jinx. The competition's marketing slogan 'Defy the Odds' could never have been more apt.

Tommy Wright

Hand on heart when the draw came out? I can tell you my exact words, 'oh shit'. That was basically it, 'we've drawn them again'. I had a little inkling though, and it goes back to the 130 years of club history – by the law of averages we're going to win this bloody cup! And why couldn't it be in my first year? I came out with the line 'you can't change history, but you can create it'. We used that in the semi-final and the final. I was also thinking that it would be in the minds of the Aberdeen players, knowing they had the Indian sign over us, that we could turn them over sometime. Why not in the semi-final? So we used all that, we said things to the players in meetings. We'd all be in one room, having a chat, and we would say 'they'll be thinking that they almost just have to turn up, they've beaten you so many times. But we know we can do better, they can't do any better.' It was just trying to plant seeds into our players' heads that Aberdeen's players may have had doubts. Sometimes it works, sometimes it doesn't.

Frazer Wright

You might have thought 'we don't want Aberdeen again because they turned us over in the League Cup semi-final'. But, at the same time, you might want another shot at them to prove that we can beat them.

Steven MacLean

Everyone was saying, 'you don't want Aberdeen', but I wasn't bothered who we got. I was just happy to be there. As soon as we got Aberdeen, everybody wrote us off and that suited us. I was happy with that. We knew within the camp that we fancied ourselves to beat them. Obviously, they had the edge over us that season, but we were confident going into the game that we could get a result. It was probably the hardest draw of the lot, but if you're going to win the cup you've got to beat good teams at some point. Yeah, I was confident. A lot of my friends and my family were thinking we were going to struggle, so I knew it would feel even better if we did get a result against them.

Nigel Hasselbaink
When the draw came out we were like 'wow, we're playing Aberdeen again'. But everyone was saying 'no, they can't beat us again'. Everyone was focused and we were determined not to lose.

Chris Millar
When we drew them again, we wanted to get revenge for that League Cup semi-final result because I felt it wasn't a fair reflection of the game. After that match, we were devastated, it was gutting. I felt we gave a good account of ourselves and we ended up losing 4-0. It was that semi-final tag for us again, the nearly men, having never quite got to a final. That was the story of my career, up to that point, as well.

Alan Mannus
I hadn't played in the League Cup semi-final because of my thumb injury, but we had done well to get into another semi-final. For me, all our potential semi-final opponents – whether it was Rangers, Dundee United or Aberdeen – are considered bigger clubs and would be expected to beat us. To me, it therefore didn't make a difference who we got in the draw, because we were going to face the same sort of task. It didn't matter. We knew if we wanted to get to the final we had to beat one of them. In cup games anything can happen, so it didn't matter that they had beaten us in the other cup semi-final.

Patrick Cregg
Getting Aberdeen, we hadn't beaten them all season. But I thought, with the law of averages, we had a chance, especially

when there is not much between teams. It's not as if they are Barcelona and we are St Johnstone. OK, they have a bigger budget and probably have a better squad or team overall, but on any given day there is nothing in it. By the law of averages, we had to beat them at some point.

Dave Mackay

At the time, when I heard the draw, I was probably thinking that was the one we didn't want, to be honest. Of the three, you would probably say Aberdeen was the one we maybe wanted to avoid, certainly after the League Cup defeat – although I think 4-0 that day was a little bit harsh. We certainly had to learn a lot of lessons from that game and make sure we cut out the silly individual errors that we made to put in a better performance.

Stevie May

I played for just under half an hour in the 3-0 semi-final defeat to Motherwell in 2011, the club's last Scottish Cup semi-final. They were up 3-0 early and I remember going on late in the game. So it was great to be back on the semi-final stage again, so soon after the League Cup defeat to Aberdeen. People were saying we didn't want to get them again, as they had won the League Cup and had put other teams, like Celtic, out of the Scottish, so it wasn't the ideal draw. But we simply had to focus on the game. We had the other tie against them to look back on, to see where we went wrong and how we could improve.

James Dunne

I had a feeling we would get Aberdeen, anyway. While I was at St Johnstone, we played them four times. We played up at their place at the start of March and they won 1-0, but we should have beaten them as we just didn't take our chances. We drew with them 1-1 in the league after the semi-final as well.

David Wotherspoon

With it being another semi-final, you thought 'we're going to get them again'. And that season we didn't really play that well against them.

Gary McDonald

The 4-0 loss was never a 4-0. We felt we were the better team in the first half and we went in 2-0 down. Jamie Langfield made a great save from Lee Croft's shot at 1-0.

Michael O'Halloran

We were due one against them. If you look at the games we played them, even in the 4-0 loss, they were generally close games.

Lee Croft

I pulled my hamstring the day before the second semi-final against Aberdeen. We were training at Celtic's Lennoxtown. I didn't know if my season was over, but I was just devastated about missing the game as it was such a big match. I had to sit in the stands.

David Wotherspoon

It was Aberdeen again and we had to focus. I remember before the game some of the experienced lads were reiterating that you don't get many chances to be in a final. They just said this could be our last one and we had to win the game. You could just tell they were right up for it and desperate to get to a final.

Brian Easton

It was a strong semi-final line-up. Over the season, we had played Aberdeen a few times and they seemed to just get an early goal, a scrappy one, and then we just couldn't break them down. But you get yourself into the way of thinking 'it's revenge time.'

Steven Anderson

As we play each other that many times anyway, and in the cups as well, they obviously thought they knew what we were like.

Tommy Wright

Away from the football, the funny thing about the semi-final was the story on the way to the game from our hotel at East Kilbride. We got everyone on the bus... and the one fault Callum has is he can't count people on the bus! Callum said everyone was on and we set off on this rainy day, got down the lane away from the hotel... but we had left our sports scientist, Colin Levey! I only have one focus on a match day – it's that the players are the most important people. So I said 'sod him' and then 'keep going' to the bus driver. Callum was going 'no, stop' and I said 'no, keep going, the only thing that matters is the players. He can't win us the game, so we'll just go.' I want preparation to be spot on – the guys think I've got OCD. But they talked me into waiting for him, so he ended up running about 600 to 800 yards down to the bus in the rain. We got him on the bus and away we went to Ibrox.

Callum Davidson

It's a long driveway going up to the hotel at East Kilbride, probably about a mile long. I tried phoning Colin and couldn't get hold of him. Tommy was saying 'just leave him, just leave him' and I said 'no Tommy, we've got loads of time'. So Tommy and I had a wee ding dong about leaving him or not, and I tried phoning him again. Tommy was obviously getting irate and the bus was then right at the end of the driveway. Tommy turned to the bus driver and said 'go' and I was trying to say 'just hold on a minute, he'll be here, he'll be here' because we were slightly earlier in our departure times given how organised Tommy likes to be! Then out the bus mirror I see this guy absolutely pegging it with his bags with his tracksuit on, running down the driveway in the rain and onto the bus!

Tommy Wright

In the lead up to the game, we simply tried to be as relaxed as we could about it, but we knew the importance of it.

Chris Millar

When Niall McGinn scored after 15 minutes it felt like the same old story, as they had started games against us that season so quickly and so well. They caught us cold a couple of times. When they went ahead again, you're thinking 'for goodness sake, here we go again.'

Alan Mannus

Maybe some people were thinking 'oh, here we go'. When you go a goal down, it's hard to come back from that, especially ourselves who don't tend to score a lot of goals compared to some other teams. For us, to win a game, we usually maybe only win by one goal or, at the very most, maybe two.

Dave Mackay

To be honest, when we did go down 1-0 you're thinking 'here we go again, it's going to be the same old script here'. Every time we played Aberdeen that season we seemed to lose an early goal and you are then chasing the game. They are a team you don't want to go behind against, because they are so quick on the counter attack. If you start pressing trying to get back into a game, they can pick you off. It's never ideal going behind to them, certainly again in another semi-final.

Brian Easton

At 1-0 down, it was like any other game – we just had to keep going.

Tommy Wright

We went 1-0 down and it was difficult. But I watched the game back and I didn't think we were as bad as what some of the pundits thought. I didn't think Aberdeen were that much better than us in the first half, but they had more control of the game. We still had a great chance with May from close range, just after Alan came off his line to make a really good block from Adam Rooney.

Alan Mannus

We just stuck at it. If they had scored another one, maybe it would have been difficult, maybe it would have changed the way the game went – but they didn't. It's my job to do that, me making a save isn't any different to anyone else on the pitch doing their job, which they all did.

Dave Mackay

I think we got a huge lift when Rooney missed that chance after Alan pulled off a great save. If it had gone to 2-0 before half-time, you've got an uphill task and you probably couldn't have seen us getting back into the game. I think for them, knowing that they should have been 2-0 up, and us knowing we could have been out of the cup, it gave us a huge lift to make sure we were still in the tie come half-time.

Michael O'Halloran

There wasn't a lot in it in the first half, and May had a wee chance just before half-time.

Stevie May

I remember when they went 1-0 up, subconsciously thinking 'oh no, early goal, here we go again'. When we got in at half-time, we just thought we might as well have a go here, go out and see what happens.

David Wotherspoon

At 1-0, we just kept on going, we thought we had nothing to

lose. I just think we grew and grew into the game. We went in at half-time and we had a right good chat, everyone was so positive about going out and winning the game. I don't think there was a negative thought in the dressing room about losing. We were always thinking positively and knew the importance of the next goal.

Frazer Wright
There were a few words at half-time. 'Macca' was going a bit loopy, getting the boys up for it to go back out and perform in the second half – and we did.

Tommy Wright
Half-time was important. We got them in and tried to be as positive as we could. But sometimes the dressing room just takes over and a wee bit of that happened in the semi-final. Just before they left, I was saying something, Callum was saying something and they were geeing each other up, almost willing each other to get out and win it. I think 'Macca' summed it up, I think it was the last thing said. I had spoken, and then he said, 'Aye, you're right gaffer, because there is no bloody way I'm going to be bloody lying on a beach in the summer knowing I've lost to this team again in a semi-final. We must get into the final.'

Steven MacLean
At half-time, I just did my usual. I had a little bit of a bite, not a go at people, but just sort of said that these opportunities don't come along very often, especially for the older ones. There was no point going out in the second half and just going under. I said we might as well go out and have a right go at them and see if we can get a result. I didn't think we performed as well as we could in the first half, perhaps it was the occasion. I just said 'let's go and have a right go and see where it takes us'. I maybe didn't say it as calmly as that, as I was just so hyped up! To be honest, you

never know, it might never happen again. It took St Johnstone 130 years to get to a Scottish Cup final. I knew a few of us were getting later into our careers and we might not get another semi-final, let alone a final.

Callum Davidson
'Macca' is actually quite hilarious – he head butts the door before he goes out. He has to be out last. He gets himself really psyched up for games. He is a great person to have in your team, a good leader on and off the pitch. You need to calm him down at times in training, he gets the red mist over him, but in the semi-final he basically had a complete desire to win the game. Since we had been beaten 4-0 in the semi-final, I think that was probably the one that was really irking us. We didn't want to get to two semi-finals and lose to Aberdeen in both. It was basically a shared belief and shared determination to win the game.

Frazer Wright
Someone needed to say something, someone needed to do something and 'Macca' stood up and did it. I think, as well, it was a case of there being 45 minutes left of a semi-final. If you go out and give it a go and you get beaten 3-0, well we were getting beaten anyway. We knew we might as well go out and give it a go.

Brian Easton
'Macca' always gees you up – it helped.

Chris Millar
I think with the characters we have, like Steven MacLean at half-time, all the boys were fired up for the second half. 'Macca' said 'this is our chance, we're not going to let this get away.'

Dave Mackay
We've got a few boys who will say their piece at half-time. The

manager comes in and he will normally speak for a few minutes, him and Callum, then they more or less leave it to the boys to sort it amongst ourselves at times, which isn't a bad thing. Boys will say things, not singling out players for mistakes or whatever, but trying to get a reaction to get the guys going, get them believing again. At only 1-0 down, you've always got a great chance of getting back into a game – no matter who you're playing. And we did. I don't know why, but it was more a case of saying 'we don't get beaten again by Aberdeen, we've been beaten enough times by them this season. We've got a chance of getting to a Scottish Cup final, which maybe some of us will never have again.' There was a huge incentive there to go out and turn the game around, which thankfully we managed to do.

Tommy Wright
Yeah, we tweaked the system, we went 4-3-3 if you like, putting Stevie May on the left, and it worked a treat. But it was down to the players – they upped their game, upped the tempo, got in their faces and made it difficult for Aberdeen.

Callum Davidson
Stevie basically drifted out to the left anyway. I think that was because we were playing on big pitches – it was just to try and get control of the ball a little bit, a foothold in the game, putting five in the midfield in a way or three up top. Our team formation was quite a flexible one and we were capable of changing a lot, the likes of O'Halloran and Wotherspoon could change as well. I think sometimes just little changes help you. I wouldn't say it was tactical genius in the semi-final – realistically it's down to the players keeping the ball. Football becomes complicated when you try and dissect it all. If you don't keep the ball, then you'll never win. When 'Mayso' went on the left, he took the full-back the other way and caused problems. He just wanted to score goals and 'Macca' took care of the centre-halves. It worked

quite well. In the second half of the semi-final, we made that wee change. Barry Robson was getting control of the ball in the middle of the park and we changed it from that.

Dave Mackay
We had a little bit of belief that we could turn it around if we got the first goal in the second half.

David Wotherspoon
Maybe in the first half we were a wee bit nervous because it was such a big game, everyone gets a wee bit nervous now and again. But in the second half, because we were chasing the game, we became calmer and pushed on.

Tommy Wright
I look at Willie Collum in the semi-final and I think why doesn't Willie referee like that all the time? Because Steven MacLean could have had a yellow card, so could Barry Robson or Willo Flood. He let the play go on, he didn't stop the game. There were fouls and he gave free-kicks, but he didn't book players, and I think that helped us. MacLean was able to play aggressively the whole game. If he had booked MacLean early on, that may have affected his performance. I don't know whether they are told to referee semi-finals differently. So there were little things that conspired for us. For the equaliser, it could have been a foul on the edge of the box for a high foot from Dunne, but he won the ball cleanly, and May's finish was brilliant – it was incredible. Then you could almost see the change on the pitch, you could see it in their eyes. They had not gone, but they were thinking 'oh sugar, they've got the momentum'.

Steven MacLean
Sometimes when you play in the bigger games, if the referee gets his cards out early, it sort of ruins the game. I thought Willie

refereed it excellently that day, especially not booking me! Willie had actually sent me off in the 1-0 defeat to Aberdeen at the start of March and it was very harsh. I remember as well having an argument with Del (Derek McInnes) in the semi-final, as he had shouted on the park to Willie, saying I should be booked. I shouted a couple of things back, telling him to mind his own business and look after his own team.

David Wotherspoon
After we scored the equaliser, you could feel them getting nervous – and because they had more fans than us they felt more pressure to win the game. For me, it felt like they started to panic a wee bit.

Gary McDonald
I didn't play in that semi-final, as I was in the stand having picked up a knee injury towards the end of March. But watching it, as soon as we got the equaliser I don't think we looked back. Their fans got very nervous, which I think then passed onto the players.

Brian Easton
When 'Mayso' scored the equaliser you realised the relief. I knew we were going to win it after that.

Steven Anderson
After we scored the equaliser, I think we were the only team winning it. I think you could see that, as their heads went down.

Michael O'Halloran
I started the game on the left, but we changed things. Stevie May liked dropping left, cutting in and shooting. The gaffer's done it a few times, just tweaked the formation in games.

Chris Millar
The boys were all fired up and we just ran over the top of them

in the second half. All the boys pushed themselves to the limit, found that extra gear. When 'Mayso' got the equaliser, you could see it in the Aberdeen players' eyes that they had sunk, and they didn't know where to go. There was nobody talking, nobody leading them, whereas we were all kind of pumped right up and the momentum was with us.

Dave Mackay
I think when it went to 1-1 you could feel on the pitch that Aberdeen just seemed to drain of energy and, possibly, belief. It was a strange feeling and we certainly looked the stronger team at that point and felt as though we could go on and win it.

Steven MacLean
Once we scored the goal, I felt so comfortable in the game. I felt there was only going to be one winner. You could sense on the pitch that they had gone, I felt. Although McGinn had a good chance with his header at the back post, I felt that we had them.

Dave Mackay
The ball came in from the far side. I don't know if it got caught up in the wind slightly but I was caught on my heels and McGinn had a free header from about six yards. Thankfully, he missed. It just shows you how little things can change games. If he had scored, then the chances are they would have gone through to the final. So you need a little bit of luck in cup runs, that's for sure, and we got a little bit in the Scottish Cup run which we probably didn't get in the League Cup.

David Wotherspoon
Seeing McGinn's chance not go in, I think it just gave us more belief that it was going to be our day and we were going to push on and get the winner.

Chris Millar

They had that chance with McGinn and when he missed you are thinking 'maybe it's our day, this is our day'. He probably should have scored, but he put it inches past the post. With things like that, you start believing that wee bit more and obviously then 'Mayso' scored his second.

Tommy Wright

Listen, we got a wee bit of luck with the header from McGinn. I still say it to this day – I don't know how he missed it after the deep cross to the back post. But our second goal was a super goal. I mean, Dave Mackay's diagonal is a great ball, Stevie's aggression and desire to win the ball, a great lay off from 'Macca', then the run, finish, celebration, wow! As May burst through, I was just looking at it, thinking 'go on hit it, hit it'. He took it early and he deceived Jamie Langfield.

Dave Mackay

For the second goal, I sent a long diagonal ball to Stevie. He nodded it in to MacLean, who played it just round the corner back into his path. It was a great goal, a great finish again from 'Mayso'.

Chris Millar

May won the header, into Macca, and then back to May who smashed it in. They had worked so well together all season. I knew then we were going to do it.

Steven MacLean

Stevie came up with two great finishes for us. You get your plaudits and headlines, like in the final because I scored a goal, but I actually thought I played better in the semi-final. The second goal was a great goal, a good move after I played him in. To be fair, it was good for Stevie as well because everybody was saying he hadn't scored against Aberdeen and their fans were giving him a bit of stick.

Stevie May
It's fair to say, given the situation, what happened and what it meant, that was probably as good as it gets, at that time. For their importance, both goals are my best strikes in a Saints shirt. It was as good a result as I had had for St Johnstone. It was just kind of meant to be that day for us. It did make it a bit sweeter as they were the ones who put us out of the previous competition. I was taking a bit of stick from their fans as well, as I hadn't scored against them that season, so it's always nice to give a little bit back.

Alan Mannus
With Stevie May playing, we felt we always had a chance and he took the goals so well, a couple of brilliant finishes. We were under a bit of pressure, but even with that, I didn't really have to make any saves in the second half. McGinn had his good chance that he put wide, sometimes they go in and sometimes they don't. We defended well apart from that.

Patrick Cregg
You just need to be fortunate and we were fortunate at times. I think our name was on the cup, to be honest. I remember being in our hotel room right before the semi-final. I was rooming with 'Mayso', and I said to him 'I genuinely think we're going to win this cup'. I couldn't see where a goal was coming from in the semi-final and then he popped up with the equaliser, and went on to get the second one as well. I genuinely felt that we could get to the final and win it, the same as when I was at Falkirk. You just get a good vibe going, especially if you get good draws along the way.

Stevie May

I roomed with Cregg before the semi-final and he said what he thought was going to happen, he had a feeling we were going to be in the final. He said 'it was meant to be, it's our year,' that kind of thing. It's not like him, but he was right.

Tommy Wright

They didn't have a chance after we went 2-1 up, that's what really pleased me. We didn't just show character to come back, we also saw the game out without any problems.

Steven MacLean

When the second goal went in, I was like 'how long is there to go?' A few of us were ready to cramp up, so there was no chance of us making extra time! We thought we better hang on!

Dave Mackay

Towards the end of the semi-final, we did have a few players cramping up, but I also felt that Aberdeen were even more tired than our players. They just looked totally drained. The last few minutes they tried to throw everything forward, punted the ball, put everybody up front, but we managed to see that through. If it had gone to extra time, I don't think they looked any fresher than us anyway. I would have still fancied our chances.

Alan Mannus

I remember at the very end, in injury time, we must have all been thinking 'just get the ball into the corner'. The ball came to Dave Mackay and he just kicked it up in the air, as high as he could almost, and it just went right down into the corner for a throw in which ended up being just perfect. It was a bit of a relief then. When the whistle went, it was just unbelievable. Aberdeen were probably favourites for the cup so, for us to upset the odds and for Aberdeen to have so many supporters there probably expecting to get into the final, it was amazing. For our fans there, what it meant to them, as well as what it meant to the players, it was fantastic. There was talk that Aberdeen fans had booked hotels for the final, it was along those lines, before they played us in the semi-final. It meant a lot for us to do it.

Chris Millar

When the final whistle went, it was one of the best feelings. For me, I think that game also answered a lot of question marks about Stevie May. Could he go to that next level? He had scored a lot of goals but he hadn't scored against Aberdeen up to that point and was taking stick from their fans, who were singing their songs about him. They certainly found out who he was after that game. Could he go to that next level? For me, it was an emphatic yes.

Stevie May

I think it was kind of written in the stars for us that day, that season. If it was meant to be, it was meant to be, and that day it was. Thankfully, it was me who managed to get the goals, on a personal level, but as a team it was great to come back and give ourselves that chance to go and play in a Scottish Cup final.

James Dunne

In the semi, Stevie came up trumps, which he did most of the time. After Aberdeen scoring in the first half and us thinking 'oh shit,' the way we came back was superb. It was mental, really, how it felt on the day, beating a side like Aberdeen who were on form at the time. It was a good win and a good day.

Callum Davidson

You ride your luck a little bit in games, they missed a couple of chances and we had a couple. In the end, it's two great goals from May, coming in off the left hand side. It was quite pleasing to see our system switch work.

Steven MacLean

Stevie was good cutting in from the left. In the semi-final, the gaffer did tweak it a bit, putting 'Mayso' out to the left. He used that tactic in big games. Even in the final, the gaffer played that card, putting him on the left, and the second goal came from there too.

Nigel Hasselbaink

It was a great feeling to beat Aberdeen, even being on the bench. It was a very close game and Stevie May scored two brilliant goals. It was a great feeling for everyone, even for us on the bench. The feeling at the end was unbelievable.

David Wotherspoon

I think we opened the beers soon after, in the dressing room.

Gary McDonald

I obviously didn't play, but I remember in the dressing room it was more a relief than a celebration amongst the boys. That season we had two opportunities to reach a final and if we hadn't taken one of them it would have been really hard to take and come back from.

Tommy Wright

We knew that the fans probably couldn't take another semi-final defeat. I think if we had lost that semi-final it would have been really difficult for Mackay and guys like him, a lot of the older players. They might have thought 'we've missed the best opportunity ever to get to a final'. Even though it was Aberdeen, it was still a semi-final. It would have been another defeat in a semi-final – it would have been so hard to get over it. It's almost like a mental barrier to get over. It would have been even harder, I think, to contest another semi-final in the future after another loss. You can't keep falling at the same hurdle all the time. I didn't mention it, but I thought it.

Callum Davidson

We showed great tempo in the second half and that's what we strive to do every game. Tommy and I can tell after 15 minutes how a result is going to be, to be honest. You can tell the tempo and from the look of the players. Our preparation is virtually always the same – we tell them to start well, start with high energy and so on. I thought the semi-final was a bit more tactical in the first half, I thought it was pretty even, although they got the goal. Aberdeen probably just shaded it and then at half-time there was just that desire and belief from us to go and win it. And the fear of losing again, that was important as well. I suppose it's like Andy Murray getting to five finals and losing and then in the sixth one he knows he can't get beaten. It was probably exactly the same mentality. But we were a group of players doing it, rather than an individual.

James Dunne

We wanted to win that semi-final so much because we knew it might be our only chance. You get that far, and you've got the likes of Celtic who are not in the competition. From when I was in Scotland, they were the outstanding team we played. I think Aberdeen turned up and kind of thought it was going to be easy, they were a bit sure of themselves, thinking they had already won the cup. It was good for the boys who had been to so many semi-finals before and lost them, guys like Chris Millar beside me in the middle of the park who played really well on the day.

Chris Millar

When Jody Morris moved on, it gave me a chance to play in the middle of the park with St Johnstone. I think I've probably been playing my best football since Jody went. It's funny how football works, because Jody was great with me. We used to travel up together, he stayed in Bridge of Weir just 15 – 20 minutes from me in Greenock, so I picked him up in the mornings and vice versa. I felt the two of us were on the same wavelength the way we like to play the game – I guess we're a similar type of player. Jody has played at a really high level so it was good to learn from him all the time, and just the way he is. He's not the tallest, but when he spoke you listened. He definitely had a presence about him within the dressing room and people listened to him.

He was a leader on the park as our captain as well, always did a lot of talking, and was always speaking to me about different aspects of my game. In a way, before I came to Saints I was a central midfielder and that's where I wanted to play. But with Jody and Murray Davidson, I played on the right and Liam Craig was usually on the left, we were often a midfield four. Jody was great for my career, I enjoyed playing with him and learning from him, but at the same time, if he hadn't been there, I'd have loved to have played in the middle of the park.

Tommy Wright
It was amazing at the final whistle after the semi-final. Anne was over, as were my brothers, nephew and sister-in-law. They were up in the stand, so it was a quick wave up to them and then out to celebrate with the players. When I look back at the photos, it was just sheer joy, pleasure and togetherness. The grins were so wide. It was just something they deserved on the day, nobody can ever take that away from them – and then they were looking at a final. The noise the fans made that day was incredible, they had suffered all those semi-final defeats, and I was delighted for them. There were pictures of people crying in the stand because we had done it. We had finally done it.

Alan Mannus
It was fantastic to beat Aberdeen. Derek McInnes signed me, he was the one who gave me my opportunity, in terms of coming over to Scotland, to get a move to full-time football. Nobody else had ever done that in my career, so I'll always owe him for

bringing me in, as well as the club. But, that said, I never played a game under Derek. He left a couple of months after I joined.

Chris Millar

For me, that semi-final said so much about 'Macca'. The work that 'Macca' did that season was important, his link play and talking Stevie May through games. The two of them linked up so well. I think Stevie's goals were a massive factor in our success, but I think 'Macca's' role, leading the line so well and taking the ball in, was superb. He is such a massive player for us and when he's been out we've always missed him. He is just such a massive influence on and off the park, the way he is, how aggressive he is on the pitch and runs himself into the ground. He and Stevie just complemented each other so well, his strength and power running in behind and his finishing, while 'Macca' is more about taking the ball in and linking the play, talking him through games. It was just a great partnership.

Steven MacLean

It was like an ideal partnership for me, because 'Mayso' was always looking to stretch the play, always running in behind. It created space for me to link up the play. If you look from the first game we played together to the last, you can see the improvement in him. He worked ever so hard, worked really hard in the gym, worked hard in training and I think he learned a lot as well. If you look at his link up play from the start of the season to the end, what a difference there was. The good thing about Stevie was that he always wanted to learn, from everybody, and he was always on the training pitch practicing new things. I think that was a big thing about him. What an outstanding season he had, some of the goals he scored were fantastic. He could score goals just himself, he didn't need good crosses or balls in to him. He used to score goals out of nothing, which was a good thing as well. It didn't really matter about the service at times.

Callum Davidson

I don't think as a coaching staff we were euphoric in the aftermath of the semi-final. We were delighted but you have to show respect to the other team and Aberdeen were very respectful of us winning. As gutted as they were, they wished us all the best in the final. I've seen celebrations in the past where people get carried away after semi-finals. We got back in the dressing room and Tommy made his point, saying there is no point getting to the final if you are not going to win it. That was the message straight away after the game. Yes, we were delighted we won because it was a tough game, but we focused from that point.

Tommy Wright

Everybody wanted an Aberdeen – Dundee United final, let's be honest, that's what they wanted, or they wanted an Aberdeen and Rangers final, they didn't want us. Even for Dundee United, it's their second derby, so nobody wanted it. But I actually thought the story was St Johnstone, the best story for football and talking about the romance of football and the cup – the best story was for St Johnstone to win the cup. The others have all won it – they are all big clubs and have their history.

Steven Anderson

We didn't over-celebrate. It was a relief, really. We had never been to the final of the Scottish Cup and we enjoyed celebrating for the fans.

Tommy Wright

Mobile phones are a great invention, I could never do without it, and I think I had something like 290 messages after the Aberdeen game. But when you change your phone, I'm hopeless, a lot of numbers I didn't know. I'm texting back 'who is this, I never stored your number?' There were people I hadn't heard from for years and it was incredible the reaction of people – people who I had played with, friends and family. I had about the same number of messages after the final.

Alex Cleland

The belief from the players in the semi-final was superb. Aberdeen were a very good side at the time, so to turn it round was really, really special. There was a really nice touch after the game from Stewart Milne, the Aberdeen chairman. We were on the bus outside Ibrox, with the buses of both teams side by side. Stewart came out of the doors at Ibrox and actually came on our bus, popped his head in, and said 'well done boys, that was a great result and I wish you all the best in the final. Go and win it now'. It was a great little touch from him. I have total respect for the man, coming on our bus after his team had been beaten in a semi-final. I thought it was a touch of class. He didn't need to do that and it was so good of him to do it. I don't think a lot of chairmen would do that after losing a semi-final.

Frazer Wright

We had a few beers back in the hotel, and some of us got a couple of days off.

As the Saints players caught their breath and realised, collectively, what they had achieved sitting in the Ibrox dressing room, word filtered through of a remarkable turn of fate. Seriously, what were the chances of the man who scored the two goals that took his side to their first Scottish Cup final having the exact date of that showdown emblazoned on his back? Having gone through 130 years of cup misfortune, who could blame the Perth punters for sensing cup final glory could be written in the stars?

Stevie May

I never had a clue about the significance of my shirt and the day of the final. It wasn't until after the game and someone said it when we were doing interviews, kind of pointed it out. I couldn't even have told you what the date of the Scottish Cup final was. I didn't know, it didn't click.

Frazer Wright
It was just after the semi-final we realised.

Steven Anderson
The press were all over May 17. It was a great omen, really. It was great for the press to get on the back of it.

Brian Easton
I thought it was unbelievable, the omen.

Steven Anderson
Maybe it was fate for us (McGinn's miss in the semi-final and then the May 17 omen). And it was about time, to be honest, we badly needed success.

Callum Davidson
That semi-final comeback, that second half, is probably the reason we won the Scottish Cup. If you are asking me 'how did we do it? It was just sheer belief and determination.' And that didn't stop at the semi-final – they all took that into the final. If we had beaten Aberdeen with a scrappy 1-0 win, we might not have gone into the final with that same belief.

6

THE FINAL COUNTDOWN

Now we stand on the precipice,
Of success we're not used to this.

'Fair Maid'
The Shrugs

THE DAY OF destiny was nearing. For all connected with Saints, it was hoped the fact that talismanic striker Stevie May wore the No 17 jersey was a sure sign the club's name was to be engraved on the famous old trophy as winners of the 2014 William Hill Scottish Cup final. So the canny T-shirt sellers thought! Off the park, thousands near and far snapped up tickets with feverish anticipation, praying the club's 130-year wait for major silverware was finally to come to an end. On the park, it was hardly surprising Saints won just one of their post-split matches, given that minds were elsewhere. However, there were creditable draws with Aberdeen and Celtic, while the significance of the 2-0 home win over cup final opponents and Tayside derby rivals Dundee United on 19 April could not be underestimated. With the curtain coming down on the league season at Inverness, preparations for the Celtic Park showdown and the biggest match in the club's history began in earnest...

Stevie May
I got used to it, the No 17 thing was everywhere in the lead up to the final. It was more the name and the date that was taking the attention, as opposed to me getting it on a personal level. I wish I'd been getting a cut of the merchandise! I've missed out

massively! The press in the lead up to the final was kind of mad – I guess that's something you expect when you get to that stage of the competition.

Tommy Wright

I didn't realise the build up to the final was going to be as long, I thought it would just be the last week. The hype about the cup final was just constant, while we also had to focus on trying to get as high up the league as possible. It was new territory for everyone at the club. I put a rallying call out early, said we wanted to take 15,000 fans to Celtic Park and the tickets sold very well.

David Wotherspoon

To be fair, there was plenty of talk about the fans and their backing for us. As the weeks went on, supporters were buying tickets and the number just kept rising.

Steven MacLean

It was a long week. I remember playing up at Inverness on the Sunday and we were shocking. You are saying to yourself before the game 'c'mon, let's just play well here and try and consolidate your cup final place.' In the back of your mind, you're also thinking 'don't get injured' but we were shocking. It was just one of those days, we didn't play well. But we came through the game unscathed, which was the most important thing.

Tommy Wright

We had made the top six again, which was great. We played Inverness on that final Sunday and we were poor. I gave them a wee bit of a rattle, a wee reminder that we didn't play as we can, but I could fully understand. So I gave them a wee get out with their minds being on the cup.

David Wotherspoon

It was just one of those days at Inverness where everyone's minds were somewhere else – but we soon focused on the final. I had sat in the stands for two finals with Hibs, so I was obviously desperate to play in a final. Tommy said to me in the build up that I would definitely be involved in the game, which sort of put me at ease a wee bit. I was just buzzing to play.

Tommy Wright

With David, I told him about 10 days before the final that he was definitely playing because I thought it was important that he knew. He must have been thinking 'this might happen again'. Deep down he knew it probably wouldn't, but I think he needed reassurance.

Steven Anderson

It was a poor result at Inverness, we didn't play well. It wasn't to be expected, as we wanted to win to go into the final with confidence high. We still had that, but at Inverness you could maybe understand why we didn't perform. We made the journey back down to Dunkeld House Hotel and it was forgotten about. We had a big week until the final.

Tommy Wright

We persuaded the chairman to spend a wee bit of money for two nights at Dunkeld! We had everything planned. We came back from Inverness, Alex was left in charge of the players and we allowed them a meal together and a couple of pints in the hotel on the Sunday night to let them relax. Meantime, the chairman, Callum, Stevie May and myself went to the Scottish Football Writers' Association dinner in Glasgow that night. Stevie won the Young Player of the Year award and we came back.

Callum Davidson

I knew nothing of a cup final week, as I had experienced none as a player! It was a long week, but if it happened again we would probably do the same. In the end, we thought we couldn't take the players away from their families for too long before the game. Sitting in hotel rooms, sometimes you get tired and bored. Going away at the start of the week was much better. It worked out perfectly, as it wasn't too long at Dunkeld. The boys weren't too bored, had a good time and relaxed.

Steven MacLean

I remember we went to the hotel and the gaffer let us have a couple of drinks to relax a bit, to settle us down. We were well warned not to have too much! There were probably about 12 of us who had a couple of drinks, more the senior ones. We had a laugh and a few beers and it sort of relaxed us for the rest of the week to come.

Frazer Wright

We had a few beers on the Sunday night, which was quite relaxed and then on Monday morning we were in the pool chilling out. I won the clay pigeon shooting too, a sharp shooter.

Gary McDonald

I thought it was good to get away to Dunkeld. Your head gets pickled a wee bit from requests you don't usually get in the lead up to a game. It's a very unique kind of week.

Liam Caddis

It was great to be part of the cup final build-up. I had been on loan at Alloa and played my last game for them the week before. I knew I wasn't going to be getting stripped for the final, but what an experience it was, just being part of the build-up. It was about team bonding at the hotel but we are close to each other anyway. It was relaxed in the build-up.

Scott Brown

The mood in the camp was quite relaxed when we were up at the hotel at Dunkeld. I think the lads were keeping their minds off the game itself. It was only a game of football and we had already beaten United three times earlier in the season, so we knew we could win it.

Gary Miller

We had a couple of days bonding and the lads were feeling really good. It was all calm to be honest, nobody was really nervous or stressed about things. We were all just sort of enjoying the mood, like being in the swimming pool, just messing about, just enjoying ourselves really and having a good bit of camaraderie. We weren't panicking or worrying about what was going to happen. I think everyone was just getting on with it and looking forward to it. Even the management, they were cycling up in the hills, and chilling out. Alex Cleland came back after crashing his bike and was OK, but everyone was just generally chilled out and having a laugh, rather than being stressed.

Tommy Wright

Callum and some of us went out on the bikes. I suffer from asthma, took it late in life, and we started on a hill! Who would do that? Start a bike ride on a hill? I got probably 600 yards up the hill and had to turn round, so me and Steve Banks just went along the river bank on a flat course. Just as well I didn't go up the hill, as Alex fell off, straight over the handlebars on the way down the hill! So we had a bit of fun, the staff out on the bikes, as well as the clay pigeon shooting. We had some interviews and photos done, it was all quite relaxed.

Callum Davidson

Tommy and Steve went on the flat bit, and Alex was trying to keep up with me and Colin Levey. We were flying down a hill and all of a sudden Alex wasn't behind us! He'd fallen off on a straight road! It was dead straight going down a slight hill and he veered onto the kerb, flew straight off into a grass banking. If we get to a final again, he's got to do the same again! He was OK, but he was obviously a bit shaken up.

Alex Cleland

When Tommy and I went round to pick up the bikes there were only two left. Callum, Banks and the others had got all the good bikes! There was one good bike left and one smaller bike. Of course, I couldn't give the gaffer the smaller bike because he would have looked absolutely ridiculous, so I gave him the good one, seniority and all. But Tommy was out for about 20 minutes and we were out for over an hour. In hindsight, we would have been better swapping bikes!

We had been up and down hills, over lumps and bumps and through little pathways. Callum had discovered it and it was a brilliant bike ride. We were near the end, only about 10 – 15 minutes to go, and we were going down this long road. I just lost my concentration on the bike and I gave myself one almighty bump. I was coming off the bike onto a grassed verge, all overgrown, and as I did I saw this massive boulder lying in the undergrowth. I was heading straight for it, but managed to break my fall with my arm just in time, so my elbow caught the full brunt of it. I thought I had done something to my elbow, but I only had a few scratches and broke my watch. The bike was OK and the helmet was fine. My face was a wee bit scratched as well, so we had a good laugh about it afterwards even though I was a wee bit shaken up. I've fallen off my bike before as I'm a keen cyclist, and I do go out quite a lot. I was a wee bit embarrassed having fallen off. The boys were saying they would get me stabilisers for my next bike, so I had to take a wee bit of a ribbing!

Tommy Wright

We also had a great photograph organised at Dunkeld with us all in our cup final suits and our nice tan brogues, after we convinced the chairman this was what you did for a cup final. I organised all the suits and the shoes, got it all sorted through my contacts! We were nicely kitted out.

Frazer Wright

We had the cup final suits, and then the gaffer told us we were getting these tan shoes. They were a nice pair of shoes – I think that's the only time I've worn them. We thought the gaffer was at it with a deal, getting 10 new pairs of shoes on the side for himself! The shoes looked good, to be fair, quite nice with the suits.

Steven Anderson

To be fair, Graeme Hart, the club photographer, put money towards the shoes.

Frazer Wright

The gaffer gave us four options to pick and the boys picked one, but we got the shoes that he wanted anyway!

Brian Easton

It was just a nice chance to give the gaffer a wee bit of stick – but we don't usually need an excuse.

Callum Davidson

Here's another story about the team photograph with the brown shoes... the problem was some shoes didn't get ordered properly, all the shoes didn't come. If you look closely Alan Lochtie, the youth team physio, had to take Alex Cleland's shoes. Alex is standing in the middle with his nice lovely shoes, and Alan has got these dirty brown shoes on. Everyone else is neatly lined up!

The gaffer was raging, he didn't like it! We eventually got all the shoes – and the gaffer probably got extra pairs. He must have got a good price as he came away with about seven or eight different pairs.

Alex Cleland
The shoes that came for me were the wrong size, so we sent them back, meaning I didn't have any shoes for the photo call. Graeme, the photographer, said it wasn't a problem and I'd get someone else's shoes and Alan could wear mine. So in the photos Alan, obviously, has my shoes on. They weren't as clean as the others and they were the total opposite colour, they were dark brown! It was a bit of a mix up but it's something to look back on – it was a brilliant, long photo. It's the only one you can notice Alan's shoes in!

Tommy Wright
We had a lovely meal on the Monday night and left Dunkeld on the Tuesday morning. We came down to the club and had a light training session on the pitch and I gave them Wednesday off.

Gary McDonald
We had the press day at the club as well and the cup was here. I remember it was great to actually see it. Personally, I had never been that close to the Scottish Cup. Seeing it, it showed me the reality of the situation and how close we actually were. For me, it really kicked in the importance of the week.

Frazer Wright
The week wasn't without its incidents for me. I was heading off for training and my wife was saying something about tickets for the final. I had practically left the house but, just as I came back in, my youngest daughter, Chloe, ran out of the living room. I knocked her and she went flying forward straight into the

radiator and split her head open. And I got the blame! I went to training and my wife took her to A&E. In all the cup final photos I've got with her, she has got this line on her head. We'll always have the memory!

Steven MacLean

I remember at the start of the week I was actually quite nervous, even though I was going to be playing my third final. I've got a Scottish Cup winner's medal with Rangers, I was on the bench in the 1-0 win against Dundee in 2003, and I played in the League One play-off final with Sheffield Wednesday in 2005. I came on and scored a penalty against Hartlepool and we won in extra time. I don't know why I had nerves. I kind of knew I was going to play from the start and I was hoping to do well – it was the biggest game of my career. I had quite a lot of people coming to watch, 50 or 60 tickets taken, so I was eager to do so well and win the cup. My sister came over from Australia to watch the game too, so I was obviously looking to win.

James Dunne

Leading up to the final, we really enjoyed it, because I think we didn't have a lot of pressure on us. The press and the pundits on TV were kind of saying Dundee United were going to win it. We had a bit of pressure, obviously, because the club hadn't won a major trophy and some of the players had missed out on semi-finals and this was their chance to go and win it. But we played them three times before the final and won them all, so I was quite confident going into the game anyway, especially with our strong defence and strikers like Stevie and 'Macca' who will get you goals. Leading up to the game, I think we had also scored four or five goals from corners, including one from 'Ando' against United in April. We knew that if we got things right on the day and we went about it the right way that we could go on and win it.

Gary McDonald

We had the *Sportscene* situation for the semi-finals, where comments had been made that motivated the boys as well. Dundee United were kind of the people's choice, the fashionable team with all the young talent, and nobody really spoke about us as potential winners throughout the whole cup competition. I think that went with us as well.

David Wotherspoon

Basically, some pundits thought it was going to be an Aberdeen-Dundee United final and they just wrote us off straight away, even before the semi-final.

Gary McDonald

Like it was a foregone conclusion – it was a bit disrespectful.

David Wotherspoon

I think they wanted those teams in the final because they were progressing better than most teams – so our story was put into the background. But I think that's what took the pressure off us, because nobody was really thinking about us. Whereas I experienced it at Hibs where everyone was like 'we've got to win the cup, we really need to win it' after not winning it since 1902. At Saints, there was not the same pressure. At Hibs, they just think it's a curse and they just want it to be lifted. There is a lot of pressure there for it.

Tommy Wright

I knew his team, (Dundee United manager Jackie McNamara). I knew he wouldn't play all his young players. Jackie and I had a little history after some verbals on the touchline at Tannadice in March. He's got his views of it and I've got mine. I knew my team. We knew how to beat them, but I still tried to maintain the fact they were favourites. I felt we should keep it as low key as possible. The players had to realise that everything we said and did that week made us feel confident without being over confident and we trusted them to go and do their jobs.

Steven MacLean

Tommy is good like that – he was clever with what he did. I think we all sort of did it, saying they were the favourites. But, I think, deep down, we all knew that if we played well on the day that we would win the game. We really fancied ourselves, but we played it down.

Gary McDonald

Personally, I felt we bullied United at times. I felt they were a very soft team to play against, full of talented young boys who will go on to have great careers. But, at that time, I just thought we had the right players to play against them. We had boys who had been about the block and knew how to win football games.

Steven Anderson

There was no pressure on us. There were a few mind games. It was a big occasion for United's young players.

Frazer Wright

We had done well against them – had beaten them three times previously without conceding – so we were confident.

Steven Anderson

I think the press were talking them up, saying their young boys were this, that and the other. They did have very good players, but they hadn't scored against us in three games and lost them all. We had the edge on them, to be honest.

Frazer Wright

We were thinking 'if we can get ahead, we can keep a clean sheet and win it'.

Chris Millar

I think, being at St Johnstone, you always kind of fly under the radar. We've had relative success in recent seasons, always progressing. For me, we were never going to be shouting our mouths off but within our dressing room, and with the manager as well, there was a massive confidence that we could go and win the game.

We seemed to have United's number over the season and everyone was talking them up, so we were more than happy with that as we just quietly went about our business. We also heard wee stories coming back from their dressing room, from boys you know, that they reckoned they were going to win. We just used it as more motivation to go and do the business and get the win. I think the gaffer was brilliant in the whole build up to the final, the way he played it with the press. He knew (Ryan) Gauld and (John) Souttar, two of their young boys, wouldn't start. I think our physical style of play and our pressing game didn't really suit them. I think that unsettled Dundee United a lot. We always felt that there was a wee soft side to them and we had to get in their faces.

David Wotherspoon

We dealt with the press, got it over and done with early. From then on in, it was a case of focusing on your own game. We just knew ourselves that we had had a good year against them, and leading into the final that was such a big positive for us. We knew that we could deal with anything they put in front of us. I think we had the experience over them, even though the final was going to be a completely different experience. I think we had the heads to keep our composure, deal with the situation and the pressure. From what we heard, they were doing things like they had won the cup already, like they were being too confident. People were saying they had places booked for showing off the trophy and presenting the trophy to people. It was motivation to win it ourselves.

Steven Anderson

The gaffer was good at taking our mind off things, and we had the press early in the week as well. I remember going to a scan for our baby and everything was fine, so that gave me something else to think about.

15 May 2014: Newsflash...
'Tim Clancy has been ruled out of St Johnstone's Scottish Cup final against Dundee United at Celtic Park. The Saints defender picked up a serious Achilles injury at training on Thursday morning which manager Tommy Wright believes will require an operation.' (*STV online*)

Tommy Wright

I named my team on the Thursday to the players, which I thought was important. I also told them I would name the subs on the Saturday morning. But we suffered a bad blow, as Tim Clancy got injured in training. He probably would have been on the bench and somebody would have missed out. It was a freak accident and I think that brought it home to the players how fragile sport is – you can be looking at a cup final and something happens. He was just walking, there was a pop and he ruptured his Achilles tendon. But I thought it was important to name the team, so that they knew and they could prepare – get their heads clear.

Tim Clancy, Defender, 30

I joined Saints at the end of February in 2014 on a short-term deal and scored in their last home game of the season against Celtic. In training before the final, I took a ball on my chest and as I took a step back it just felt like somebody kicked me or had fired a ball off the back of my leg. It was sore and I asked Dave Mackay if somebody had tackled me and he said 'no'. I said 'well I have snapped my Achilles then'. It was just a freak accident, but I knew it was serious as soon as it happened. It was gutting to miss the final.

Callum Davidson

We kind of knew the team, with one or two question marks, probably the biggest decision being over O'Halloran or Croft.

Frazer Wright

Tommy had spoken to a few boys about who was playing, but we had a good idea what the team was going to be. I don't think there was much he could change because we had done so well in the semi-final.

Steve Banks

By the time the final came along I was back to being player-coach and helping Alan in any way I could to prepare for the game. We stuck to the same pre-match routine and I was training and coaching as usual in the build-up. It has been great working with Alan. He has probably been the most consistent player at the club in my time here. I've been fortunate to work with good keepers who want to work hard and improve.

Chris Iwelumo

For the final, we kind of knew what the starting XI was going to be, so everyone was trying to work out who would be on the bench. To be fair, in the week building up to the final, everyone was on it in training; everyone was fighting for a place. Obviously, Tim Clancy took a bad injury two days before the final, which was so unlucky for him. I really felt for him. He had performed so well in the 3-3 draw with Celtic, the final home match of the season, but it was just one of those things. We had no idea what the bench was going to be until the gaffer actually said it in the team meeting on the Saturday morning.

Gary Miller

I think we knew, if there weren't any injuries, the gaffer was going to go with the team that had done well in the semi-final.

So it was a case of the other boys trying to make sure they were on the bench, or trying to push for a spot to get on off the bench. I was pleased to be on the bench. Luckily for myself I had been involved in the Scottish Cup final before with Ross County (2010), so I knew it was a big occasion.

Tommy Wright

I think my biggest decision was at left midfield, whether to go with O'Halloran or Croft. We went with O'Halloran in the end, before switching him to the right during the final and Wotherspoon played on the left. I spoke to Lee about it.

Lee Croft

I was just gutted. It's one of those things in football when you are playing, then you are not playing and Michael (O'Halloran) came in and did really well from then on. The wing places are competitive here and it keeps you on your toes. The hamstring was fine, as I was back for the last couple of league games. I was at least pleased to be on the bench, to be part of it.

Gary McDonald

I thought my season was over in March when I got my knee injury. I thought that was it for me, I was gutted. But as the weeks went on and the cup final got nearer and nearer, I thought I might have a wee chance of making it. I knew I might never get the chance again for a cup final. I did everything I could as I had never been to a cup final. I was determined to get back fit and thankfully I did, a few weeks before. I felt reasonably match fit going into it, but knew I wouldn't start the game as I hadn't played enough football and the boys had been doing really well. I was just delighted to be involved, to be on the bench and be part of it, to be honest.

Tommy Wright

It was a long time from the Sunday post-game. On the Thursday,

I had commitments with the cup at a local school and that's when I was getting a bit bored with the press. I was genuinely getting bored with it all as it was the same questions. I found it tough. The press commitments are demanding and, in the end, I was glad when Friday morning came and we were on the bus on the way down to our hotel.

Steven Anderson
The preparation was exactly the same later in the week as for the semi-final – the hotel at East Kilbride and training at Celtic's Lennoxtown.

Tommy Wright
We knew how we were going to play and we had one final session left at Lennoxtown. Our training was short and sharp, not worrying too much about them. We had already played them four times in the season so we knew them inside out. Neil Lennon (former Celtic manager) was very good letting us have Lennoxtown again. At the hotel, I had to have the same room I'd had for the semi-final, because of these wee superstitions you get. It's that OCD again! I think Callum was in the same hotel room as well.

Chris Millar
The gaffer tried to do everything the same as the semi-final with our preparation. We went to Lennoxtown and did our pre-match, getting use of the facilities, and went to the same hotel. Everybody stayed with the same partners. I roomed with 'Macca'. The preparation couldn't have gone any better, it was spot on. You just felt it building, like this was our time. The biggest thing for me was the semi-final. Once we got to the final, I just always felt that day would take care of itself and so it proved.

Tommy Wright
At Lennoxtown we wanted to do one final session on shape

and we told the players we would do that. But Callum came in and said because it was the end of the season there was no pitch marked out. He said 'what do you want me to do, will I mark it out in cones?' I said 'no, that looks amateurish, just leave it, we'll talk about it and go over set plays. I'll tell them we were going to work on shape, but you don't need it, you know how to beat them, you're experienced and you don't need reminded'. That comes back to the trust we had in them. We went out and the pitch actually was marked, but you could hardly see the lines. We just did a light session, a few wee games and set plays.

Callum Davidson
I remember speaking to the groundsman at Lennoxtown and he said they were about to rip all the pitches up at the end of the season. But he got a message from Neil Lennon and he said 'no, leave one pitch, St Johnstone are coming down the week after the season finishes.' So they actually kept a pitch for us, hence the reason there were no real markings. Basically, all the other four pitches were ripped up and getting reseeded for the start of the next season, but they had left their main pitch for us to train on (on the Friday). I thought that was absolutely fantastic of them and we obviously can't thank them enough, they were brilliant. It was great preparation for the boys.

Liam Caddis
Most of the boys had never been in a final before but knowing we were playing a team we had already beaten helped us prepare. We knew we could get the better of them on the day.

Chris Millar
I don't really get to bed early the night before a game. I often stay up until about 12 o'clock. You have so much energy buzzing about you and you just try to contain it. 'Macca' was like 'Right, 'Midge', get yourself to bed and compose yourself, make sure you

are right'. I remember waking up and feeling so emotional, even before a ball was kicked. I was reading through messages and felt tears welling up, because it means so much to your family as well. The emotion on the morning of the final was pretty overwhelming and a couple of times 'Macca' turned away as I was getting teary and a ball hadn't even been kicked yet! I just had to compose myself and made sure I didn't release that energy too quickly.

Scott Brown
With the subs named on the Saturday morning, it was disappointing that I wasn't on the bench because I had played against Celtic in the 3-3 game and thought I had done quite well. I thought that might have given me a chance of getting on the bench but it wasn't to be.

Gary Miller
I was on the bench, but I had a bit of an agenda for myself. I had reached the final four years previously with Ross County and it was Dundee United who beat us then. So, for myself, I had a wee bit of wanting to get my own back and win it this time. It was a bit gutting that day with County.

Tommy Wright
We did all our preparation at the hotel, did the team talk, so when we got to the ground it was basically about getting themselves ready. I couldn't tell you what I said in the team talk, it wasn't planned, but I remember Callum saying 'where did you get that from?' I said 'I don't know – we just started talking'. You get into why we are here, why we are doing it, like for our families. I do remember how I finished the team talk. I said 'this cannot be enough – it cannot be enough just getting to the final. It's not enough for me – it's not enough for you and your families. This cannot be the end. We cannot get to here and let it pass. We just

cannot.' That's when I said 'you can't change history, but today you can create it'.

Callum Davidson

After the bus story for the semi-final at the hotel, I said 'we'll need to make Colin run for the bus again as we leave'. Tommy was like 'oh, we can't do that, we can't do that,' but he still made him run a little bit, this time with his suit on! That's why we didn't make him run down so far! He ran 50 yards or so down the road and jumped on the bus. I don't think you can change these things!

Tommy Wright

We drove the bus down the road again, and there was Colin running to get it! Another wee superstition! We didn't make him run over 600 yards this time, but we did the same again.

Chris Millar

I didn't even notice all that, as on the bus I put my own music on and was starting to prepare mentally. You get loads of messages, and I got some from my mum and dad, and my brother, so I was reading all of them. My mum had sent a message about an R. Kelly song, 'I Believe I Can Fly'. I was listening to that on the way, and my brother had also messaged about the Elbow song, 'One Day Like This', so I was listening to that as well. These are the things that go through your head when you are travelling, so I didn't even notice Colin had been told to run again to make the bus. You're in your own wee zone and you're just trying to prepare for the game.

Stevie May

I don't think I felt nervous. I think it was more excitement knowing you were going to be playing in such a big event in Scotland. It was a winnable one. I think a lot of teams over the years had been getting to finals against the Old Firm, when you were expected to lose, but for it to be a Tayside derby and against a team we had beaten three times that season, we went into it with a lot of confidence and belief. I did genuinely believe going into the final that we were going to win.

Dave Mackay

We definitely knew we could win it. There was a feeling amongst everybody that this was our chance, but you have to go out and prove it on the day. Aberdeen had a great record against us up until the semi-final, so our record against United really counted for nothing in a one-off cup game. But we certainly felt that season we had the measure of them, having won three straight games against them without conceding. We felt we could score against them, so we certainly felt confident without being arrogant and thinking we just had to turn up to win it. We had to prepare right, as we always do, come out flying from the start and give ourselves a great chance.

7

DAY OF DESTINY

I dream we'll go up to lift the Scottish Cup,
Perth St Johnstone, My Fair Maid.

'Fair Maid'
The Shrugs

17 May 2014, Celtic Park
Scottish Cup Final: St Johnstone 2, Dundee United 0

Mannus; Mackay, Anderson, Wright, Easton; Wotherspoon
(McDonald), Millar, Dunne, O'Halloran (Croft); MacLean, May.
Goals: Anderson 45, MacLean 84.

*THE WAIT WAS finally over. 17 May 2014; the day to be
forever woven into St Johnstone FC's fabric. A first Scottish Cup
final appearance in the club's 130-year history, over 15,000
tickets sold for the showdown and even a ballad penned for
the occasion by a couple of local musicians. Not bad for a club
regularly put down for its lack of fan base and fervour.*

*The city of Perth had been positively purring in eager
excitement for weeks, cup final day counted down like feverish
children anticipating Christmas morning. They left in their
busloads for the chance to finally witness history; the chance for
generations of supporters to savour one of the best days of their
lives. For most of the club's long and trophy-less existence, those*

fans had clung to a dream. Suddenly, it was their chance to see it fulfilled; a chance that may not come again; a rare chance against a non-Old Firm side on the biggest Scottish stage. After so long on the outside looking in, for so long unrewarded for their financial prudence, it was a day like nothing else the club had experienced since it was formed by a band of cricketers in 1884. The patience of the Saints was to finally be rewarded.

Tommy Wright

I hadn't realised the significance of May 17 until well past the semi-final! How we came to giving Stevie the No 17 shirt at the start of the season is incredible. I don't know why we gave him No 17 – he had never had a number before. You draw up your squad list at the start of the season and you put them in. But with someone like Stevie, a striker, he might have been given No 27, or No 18, because some players, if they are not No 9, they want a multiple of 9. That's what some players do if they don't get the number that they want. I don't know how he got 17. He didn't have any qualms about it as I think he was just happy to play. I should say I looked at the cup final date, but I didn't! There were all these little superstitions flying around, and I was thinking 'listen, this is going to be our year'. The fact the final was on May 17 wasn't going to win us the final, you have to go out and do it, but it was in the back of my head.

Callum Davidson

It's best not to give the opposition any motivation – all you can do is praise them a little. Tommy probably did it slightly differently with the younger lads at United, tried to put a bit more pressure on them. Whether right or wrong, it doesn't make any difference in the end. I think he was always very complimentary towards them. We knew what we had to do. We realised United are a good team, very good at counter attacking – they had players who could really open you up with their pace – so we knew if we gave them space we would be in trouble. That was how we set up our game plan, to counter that.

Gary Miller

The lads were buzzing on the way to Celtic Park. There were a few nerves from the team that you could sense, just because of the occasion, but there was a confidence about the lads, having beaten United three times out of four that season. We knew we could do well against them and it would, at least, be a close game. The chance to win a cup doesn't come along often. I think we knew it was a great chance for us to win it. United had won it recently (2010), and their young players had been highlighted, but we knew that, over the season, we had a better win ratio against them so we were very confident in ourselves and our game plan.

David Wotherspoon

I was actually a bit gutted the game wasn't at Hampden, as everyone wants to play at Hampden in a Scottish Cup final. I came on for Hibs against Aberdeen in the 2012 semi-final and it was just such a great atmosphere. Going back to face Hearts in the final, even though I didn't play, the atmosphere was just incredible. I thought it would be nice to play there again, especially having missed out.

Michael O'Halloran

I thought it was better at Celtic Park. Personally, I think it's the best stadium in Scotland. At Hampden you are so far away from the fans, with the track round it, and I just think there's more of an atmosphere with the fans on top of you.

Gary McDonald

I'd agree with David. Growing up, you watch the finals every year and you see people going up the steps at Hampden to pick up the trophy. It's in your mind that you would love to do it one time. It was different at Celtic Park, but it didn't take any gloss off the day. You wait so long for a cup final and something like that was never going to affect the occasion for us. I remember the wee bit of rain on the day as well, which I thought was weird. As a kid watching cup finals, it always seemed to be sunny!

Michael O'Halloran
We watched a DVD on the bus on the way to the stadium, a little motivational thing from the gaffer. It was clips of all of us from games throughout the season.

Gary McDonald
I remember the bus driver took us the longest way ever to get to Celtic Park! I think, at one point, the gaffer's head was ready to go. He wants everything to be done on schedule and I think we were running a wee bit behind with the traffic. The next thing, we got a police escort to get us there!

Tommy Wright
I felt that sense of fate again. On the journey to Celtic Park we passed John Wright Sports Centre – my dad's name.

Brian Easton
I was quite chilled on the day until we arrived at the stadium on the bus and saw all the fans. We didn't expect 15,000 fans, so it was amazing. United had a great support too and the stadium looked fantastic.

Steven Anderson
People who weren't even St Johnstone fans came along. They knew somebody who was a Saints supporter and they wanted to enjoy the occasion.

Brian Easton

I had to get something like 40 tickets organised, the lads were all the same. James McCarthy and James McArthur, my former Hamilton teammates, came up to support me, so it was great to have the backing of family and friends.

Michael O'Halloran

You realise it's a slightly big deal when you get there and walk around the pitch pre-match. You're thinking 'now it's time.'

David Wotherspoon

We weren't really surprised at United's team selection. It was pretty much the way the gaffer had prepared it really. It was as if he had read Jackie McNamara's mind. Ryan Gauld was on the bench, as he had been in March against us, while Jackie quite liked to play (Ryan) Dow against us. To be fair, he had played well against us a couple of times.

Tommy Wright

Our plan was to make the pitch as tight as possible when we didn't have the ball and expand it when we had it. We worked on pressing the life out of them, to try and stop them playing. When I saw the United team there were no surprises for me, none at all, but Jackie probably knew our team. It made things easier, as we knew who was marking who at corners, as we had worked on that. A wee thing they did do was play Stuart Armstrong a bit narrower, which actually helped us. I think if Armstrong had stayed wider it would have caused us more problems. I think he played in off Nadir Ciftci almost too much.

Alan Mannus

I was fortunate to win the Irish Cup four times at Linfield, and I also won trophies at Shamrock Rovers. In fact, Tommy was my goalkeeper coach when I was about 19 at Linfield. Eventually

I ended up moving to Shamrock Rovers where Tommy was also goalie coach, which was one of the main reasons I wanted to go there, to work with him again. We didn't have the kind of crowds as for the Scottish Cup final, but I was fortunate to have been involved in cup finals with those two teams and won them before. It probably helped me on the day against Dundee United. I think the largest crowd I'd played in front of in a cup final was 30,000 or so with Shamrock. It wasn't completely new for me, but it was amazing to see so many fans from both teams, but especially ours when you walked out and saw how much blue there was. It was something special.

James Dunne
My mum and dad, Janet and John, have got one of the club's photo books from the final, because unfortunately they missed it as they were on holiday. My dad was devastated about it. They'd booked a holiday to Asia when I was at Stevenage so they obviously didn't think I was going to be playing, or even getting into a final. They went on holiday, but I had other family members there on the day, like my girlfriend, so it was nice. My dad was unhappy that he missed it, because they were on a flight going somewhere else at the time of the final. They were doing a little trip, going to a few places, Malaysia, China and Dubai. My dad was even thinking about paying for a flight back wherever they were, but I told him it was too much money so he left it in the end.

As tense Saints fans started to take their seats – preparing to strap themselves in for an inevitable rollercoaster ride – the club's manager was a picture of relaxation, calmness personified. Yet, perhaps you could understand Wright's relaxed state. After all, he had worked so hard to reach the showpiece stage in Scottish football and, rightly, he was savouring every moment.

Brought up as part of a working-class family in Ballyclare, just north of Belfast, Wright was a cross-country runner who only took up goalkeeping at the age of 19. After four years of limited first-team opportunities at Linfield, a surprise opportunity to sign for Newcastle led to an injury-hit career. His managerial career was no quicker in gathering momentum, before his big break at Saints, initially as No 2 to Steve Lomas. His last club, Lisburn Distillery, were in administration when he led them to victory in the Irish League Cup. In a wonderful show of solidarity, eight of his former colleagues attended Saints' semi-final win against Aberdeen.

Tommy Wright

I've always been brought up to think that there's nothing wrong with hard work. I've had to do it in my career because I didn't have that background where I was a schoolboy international. I was 19 when I took up goalkeeping. When I went over to Newcastle, I was probably better known as the 'Ballyclare Barman' than a goalkeeper. But I became an international through hard work and a stubborn belief in myself.

It had already been a wonderful season for his Perth charges, perhaps beyond Wright's wildest dreams. If knocking Rosenborg out of the Europa League proved a headline-grabbing start to his tenure, then reaching the semi-finals of the League Cup, the final of the Scottish Cup and finishing in the top six for the third season in a row was rather impressive for a debut dugout season, too. Now he was seeking the icing on the cake – the world's oldest national trophy – and he sensed he had all the ingredients to achieve it.

Tommy Wright

I was very relaxed before the game, thinking 'what's going to be is going to be'. I remember working under Ossie Ardiles at Newcastle. We were a young team, we were struggling, and he came in at the end of a game, in his broken English and said 'will I get a machine gun out and go rattata rattata and shoot all of you? No, it's only a game of football. When you lose it, you go home, you will see your family, you will go to sleep and wake up the next morning. So, as long as you can do that, what is there to get upset about?'

I also remember the day of my wedding. My uncle Charlie was panicking and my dad was panicking, but I was relaxed. I've always sort of had that relaxed outlook on things, like whatever is going to be is going to be. I still hurt – I hate losing, absolutely hate losing, but it's not the end of the world. To be honest, I was probably more relaxed in the final than I was in the semi-final.

There is a photo of me and Paul Smith in the dugout before the final. The lads thought I got a free pair of shoes for the final, but I didn't, I got a free pair of socks, and they were a red / pink colour. Paul and I were sitting relaxing, before the photographer, Graeme Hart, came along and I started showing him my socks. It wasn't a show, it was just who I am. It wasn't deliberate, I was so relaxed. I did an interview with Chick Young for the BBC and I was making jokes. I wanted to enjoy the experience. But I think what made me so relaxed was that I trusted my players. I trusted them. I thought this was our time.

The clock ticked towards 3pm and the players made their entrance to thunderous noise; Celtic Park a glorious contrasting picture of blue and white and tangerine. It was a fabulous atmosphere, with almost 50,000 watching on in eager anticipation.

Dave Mackay

Steve Lomas gave me the captaincy when Jody (Morris) moved on in 2012. It was the stuff of dreams leading the boys down the tunnel for the final. As a young boy, you dream about playing in those games, but to actually lead the team out was a special moment. It was a proud moment for me and I'm sure for my family, as well.

David Wotherspoon
To see over 15,000 St Johnstone fans when we came out of the tunnel was just incredible.

Murray Davidson
Tam Scobbie and I missed the final – and it was the hardest day of my career watching the lads. No one likes watching games anyway, but missing out on a final was painful. I wasn't sure how I would be. To be honest, when that first whistle went I didn't want to be there. You've been watching the build-up, the whole occasion, but you feel helpless. Despite the manager's best efforts, you don't feel part of it when the game gets going. The gaffer and everyone else had us involved right up to the Saturday of the final, but when the game started it was hard to take.

Steven Anderson
When you're in the game, after the first whistle goes, you don't think about the chance to make history. It's only really at the start when you feel a bit of pressure, a bit of nerves.

Frazer Wright
Once you are concentrating on the game, even the noise disappears. It's only when there are breaks in the play that you notice things. I think United started the better side and then we came into it.

Chris Millar
I felt in the first five to 10 minutes it was frenetic, it was high tempo. I was just trying to get a touch of the ball to bed in with wee simple passes. The way Dundee United play, they are quite

an attacking team so we had to be wary not to over commit. With me and James Dunne in central midfield, one of us always had to sit and not try and get too far forward, letting the wider boys, the full-backs and our two in attack use the space.

Tommy Wright
There wasn't a great deal in the first half. We started well, controlled it and had some chances. Dunne forced a fine save from (Radoslaw) Cierzniak with his half-volley from long range and Wotherspoon then saw his close-range effort from a free-kick blocked. We had worked on that free-kick because we knew they never put anybody on the outside of the free-kick. David made his run and the end man split off the wall, with the ball breaking into his path – but his shot rebounded into Cierzniak's arms.

Steven Anderson
It was a close game. I remember the moment in the middle of the penalty area just after 25 minutes. The ball hit off Frazer, then James, and the ball was bouncing around, neither of them would clear it until Alan picked it up! I remember Frazer laughing after it happened! Gavin Gunning then had a header wide before we rode our luck a little...

32 mins 'It's Dow! It's off the post from Ryan Dow...! Such a good move from United.' (*Sky Sports*)

Gary McDonald
It looked in, to be fair. From the dugout, it looked in. I don't know how it didn't go in. My heart skipped a beat, massively. It was just a massive relief, as obviously the first goal in a cup final is huge. If United had got it, it might have been a completely different game. So to get away with that at that time was huge.

Dave Mackay

Dow's chance was actually a little bit lucky from their point of view, although you can't really see it on the TV. Andrew Robertson crossed the ball and it took a little nick off my head to put it straight into the path of Dow. But after that, obviously, we got really lucky. It hit the post and could easily have hit Alan and gone back in.

Alan Mannus

I dived, stretched and didn't get to it. I saw it hit the post and saw it come back. I thought it was just going to clip my back, as I could see that it was coming in that direction. Obviously, I could only look at it so far before it went behind me and I didn't feel it hit me! When I turned around, I saw that the ball had stayed out and we had got it clear. It was a huge relief, obviously.

Frazer Wright

Dow thought he had scored and was almost away celebrating. He ran the other away. If he had watched the ball, seen it hit the post, he could have probably got the rebound.

Brian Easton

He just kept running, instead of running towards the ball.

David Wotherspoon

As soon as it came out off the post, I was thinking 'it's going to be our day now'. The way the ball bounced back he might have been able to run in and finish it, but he was going away thinking it was in.

Callum Davidson

I was right behind it. It's in until you see the spin on the ball and it's got that chance of missing. It was very fortunate for us because that could really have changed the match.

While it has to be remembered football is just a game, it can also stir the emotions like no other sport. After the win over Aberdeen in the semi-final, Tommy Wright had looked to the heavens at Ibrox. It was a pause for thought; a few seconds of contemplation; to think of loved ones. Twenty years previously, he and his wife, Anne, had lost their son, Andrew. He was only five. He had been born eight weeks premature with severe disabilities. "He couldn't talk but he could, if you know what I mean, with his eyes, with his smile," recalls Wright. "Eventually it got too much for him. He was such a fighter." In the final, Andrew again flashed into his head.

Tommy Wright

I think any person who loses anybody always carries a part of them in their heart. Andrew is always with me. There are days when maybe the ball hits the post and I think 'he is helping me there'. There can be little things, sentimental things. I remember in my playing career, when I came back after three years being out injured. I was playing for Northern Ireland against Germany and Jurgen Klinsmann had a header, which hit one post and went across the goal. Why I never went for it I'll never know, but I turned round and it hit the other post and came back. It's probably nothing, but you think 'well maybe that was Andrew helping me out'. And we had two off the uprights in the cup final. After the first one, as soon as it hit off Dow's foot, I thought 'oh no, this is in'. But it hit the ground and spun to my right as I was looking at it, taking it away from Alan and onto the post. Initially, it looked like it was just going to bounce and go in. You start to think then, along with May 17, 'is it our day?'

Steven MacLean

We started the game well. They made some good blocks, and we had a couple of corners. I felt comfortable, but they were

Stevie May sprints away after scoring at McDiarmid Park to help take the scalp of Rosenborg in the Europa League in July 2013. *Graeme Hart*

Defender Frazer Wright nods home the second goal from close range in the 4-0 fifth round win at Forfar. *Graeme Hart*

Gary McDonald takes the acclaim after his early strike in the quarter-final triumph at Raith Rovers. *Graeme Hart*

Steven Anderson roars his delight having clipped home to seal a 3-1 last-eight success at Stark's Park. *Graeme Hart*

That man Stevie May, the two-goal hero in the semi-final comeback victory over Aberdeen at Ibrox. *Graeme Hart*

Having tasted collective semi-final defeat so often, (left to right) Steven Anderson, Frazer Wright, Chris Millar and Dave Mackay savour the winning feeling. *Graeme Hart*

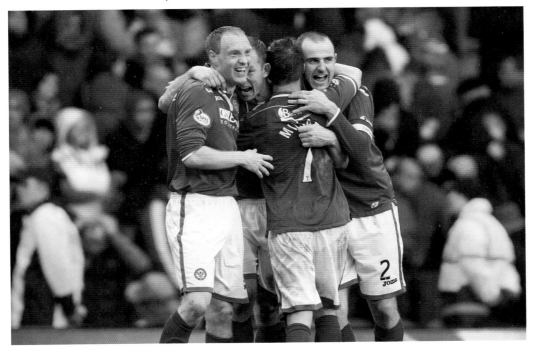

Tommy Wright beams with pride after taking the club to the Scottish Cup final for the first time. *Graeme Hart*

Suited and booted, the St Johnstone squad at Dunkeld. Can you spot Alan Lochtie's slightly different shoe colour far right?! *Graeme Hart*

Do you like my socks? Tommy Wright and Paul Smith share a relaxed pre-cup final giggle. *Graeme Hart*

Tommy Wright soaks up the atmosphere on the Celtic Park pitch ahead of the biggest game in the club's history. *Graeme Hart*

(From left to right) Alan Mannus, Dave Mackay and Tommy Wright focus on winning the famous silverware. *Graeme Hart*

Steven Anderson celebrates his opening cup final goal with Frazer Wright, Steven MacLean and Dave Mackay, as Stevie May's famous No 17 shirt wheels away. *Graeme Hart*

A delighted James Dunne leaps on Steven Anderson and his team-mates after the defender's goal just before half-time. *Graeme Hart*

Steven MacLean beats Radoslaw Cierzniak to prod home the decisive, late second goal in the cup final. *Graeme Hart*

Sheer jubilation from MacLean after sealing the historic triumph. *Graeme Hart*

Scottish Cup winners 2014! The squad begin the celebrations.... *Graeme Hart*

The blue and white ticker tape adds to the party atmosphere. *Graeme Hart*

Steven MacLean savours the moment with his children, Luke and Ruby. *Graeme Hart*

Midfielder Chris Millar parties with his kids on the park, Ellie and Sophia, and nephew, Rhys. *Graeme Hart*

The winning management trio of Callum Davidson, Tommy Wright and Alex Cleland. *Graeme Hart*

Assistant manager Callum Davidson with his daughters, Carrie and Eilidh. *Graeme Hart*

Back in the dressing room, goal heroes Steven Anderson and Steven MacLean enjoy their moment. *Graeme Hart*

Party time! *Graeme Hart*

Brilliant bus selfie from Frazer Wright on the celebratory return journey to Perth. *Graeme Hart*

(From left to right) Lee Croft, David Wotherspoon and Stevie May enjoy Sunday's bus parade. *Graeme Hart*

A proud Tommy Wright holds aloft the trophy to the cheers of thousands on the streets. *Graeme Hart*

Perth party! *Graeme Hart*

It's a dog's life. Tommy Wright with Winston, born on 17 May. *Graeme Hart*

obviously going to have periods in the game when they would do well. The cross from Robertson and the flick from Dow, it was a great finish, and it was unlucky to hit the post and come straight past Alan. For me, I wasn't actually thinking 'is this going to be our day?' at the time, as I was concentrating on the game.

Brian Easton
Sometimes I felt I had so much space on the left-hand side. It surprised me sometimes the way they played and we did take control of the game.

Frazer Wright
That was if we could get the ball through all the ticker tape down the left of the pitch in the first half!

Brian Easton
Thankfully they cleaned it off, as we had a couple of good attacks down the left, winning a corner from that side for our first goal.

45 +1 min 'It's Wotherspoon's corner... Cierzniak struggling... Steven Anderson scores! St Johnstone have the lead in their first-ever Scottish Cup final... and it comes from the man who has spent a decade with the Saints.' (*Sky Sports*)

Tommy Wright
We hadn't specifically worked on their keeper (Cierzniak), but we had worked on the back post area, because 'Ando' had scored two goals from there during the season. We had caused them problems at the back post, and other teams had caused them problems from set plays. I thought they were vulnerable at the near post, as well.

Michael O'Halloran
For United, it must have been like 'oh, here we go again, we're down to them again'.

Alan Mannus

The header from 'Ando' was the perfect time to get a goal as it didn't give them a chance to come back at us. It was right in front of their supporters as well. Going into the second half, we knew we were in a good position. If we could keep a clean sheet we would win the cup.

Steven Anderson

We scored at the right time. I scored an almost identical goal against them at home in April. Keith Watson was marking me then, as well. To be honest, I don't know what the keeper was doing. My run was mainly to go to the back post, and I had scored a couple of goals in the weeks before. The keeper came and missed it and I got above Watson to steer a header home (his fourth goal of the season).

David Wotherspoon

'Ando' always says to me when I'm taking a corner 'over hit it, over hit it' because I'll always be at the back post. He said that to me in general during the season, every time I took a corner. So I aimed to go for the back post, because their keeper (Cierzniak) had also been caught out in the game at Perth when 'Ando' scored a header. Stevie May also scored the winner against them at Tannadice in March when the ball went through the keeper's legs. We tried to put the keeper under pressure and he basically flapped at the corner and 'Ando' put in another good header.

Callum Davidson

We had worked on set pieces. I really believe that if you put the ball in the right area you can go and attack the ball. If the ball isn't in the right area, you're never going to score. David played a fantastic ball in. I'm sure he was trying to hit front post, but hit the back post (!), and we always send 'Ando' around the back. It's the first time I've seen 'Ando' happy! He is normally pretty happy when we are running and there are no balls out. He smiles. Once we get the balls out, he becomes a miserable old sod. Seriously, it was a fantastic ball for the goal.

Chris Millar
We always felt that set pieces would play a big part in the final. The gaffer had been saying it all week, identifying exactly where we could cause them problems. It was a great ball in from David and 'Ando' popped up at the back post with a great header. We had a few chances before that as well, like Dunne's effort, so we were steadily building. But, obviously, the timing of the goal, basically the last action of the first half, was perfect. It was a great time to get a goal – you couldn't have picked a better time to score. I think they looked a little shell-shocked.

Tommy Wright
What a time to score, as they couldn't do anything about it, they couldn't respond. They went in despondent, as the one team you don't want to go 1-0 down to is us. That was our 23rd clean sheet of the season. That's often forgotten, but maybe not by all people. Stevie and 'Macca's' goals quite rightly get highlighted, but we had 23 clean sheets out of 50 games. That's some record. Coming off at half-time in the final, if I was Dundee United, I'd have been thinking 'oh no, how do we get back into it against this team?'

Lee Croft
We scored at a good time just before half-time – perfect.

Gary McDonald
We were that kind of team that season. If we could get our noses in front, we always felt confident of a clean sheet.

Chris Millar
As soon as the half-time whistle went, all the boys went straight

up the tunnel. There was no kind of hanging about on the pitch. It was a great half, but it was a case of doing it all again and refocusing. We were just trying to stay calm, weren't getting carried away, and got ready to go again. There was a real focus.

Steven MacLean

In any game, scoring just before half-time is a great time to score, especially in a final. The gaffer's team talk probably changed, and I think he just had to calm us down. We were doing his team talk for him. He just settled us down, as we were all hyped up. He was telling us not to just sit in on our lead in the second half, therefore inviting pressure on to us. He set us about our business again.

Steven Anderson

In the dressing room at half-time it was a case of keeping focused. We knew if we kept a clean sheet we would win. Things were said that needed to be said and we were in the right frame of mind.

David Wotherspoon

I was buzzing at half-time. I was actually trying to calm down.

Tommy Wright

We normally let them have a minute to themselves at half-time. They were all saying 'we've got to do this – a clean sheet will win the game.' They were also saying what they normally say like 'keep working hard, deny them space.' Then we sat down and we said 'right, this is what you've done. You've given yourselves an unbelievable opportunity. That is it. What you must do is quite simple, keep doing what you've been doing. We don't need to change anything.' If we had to make a change, they knew what it would be – they knew Stevie May would go on the left if we had to make a tactical change. We had denied them opportunities, OK every team is going to get a chance, but it wasn't like backs to the wall. We had played in the right areas, and we had to continue to be confident on the ball, keep passing it and not panic with long balls out of defence as the ball comes straight back. We just had to keep going. It was nice and calm at half-time, it was collective, and they went out for the second half.

50 mins 'Ciftci! Oh and Mannus just about kept it out. How close can you get?' (*Sky Sports*)

Chris Millar
The Ciftci free-kick usually goes in. I thought back to the McGinn chance in the semi-final and again you're thinking 'maybe it's meant to be, maybe it's our time.'

David Wotherspoon
Again, I was thinking, 'this is going to be our day.'

Alan Mannus
It was a good free-kick. I remember being in the air, diving for it, and you know sometimes when you're diving, you can only dive and stretch as far as you can. You just think 'I'm not getting to this, I can't reach it.' I knew that I wasn't getting to it in the air. I could see it hit the bar and then it just come down behind me. Again, I was thinking, 'it's going to hit me and go in here' because that is usually what happens. I landed, and I just remember the feeling of it hitting me and I thought it was going to go in.

These sort of things tend to happen in slow motion in your head, but it obviously goes so quickly during the game or if you are watching it live or on TV. But, whenever you are involved, it goes in slow motion. So I had the feeling of the ball hitting me, sort of underneath my body, and then looking over and seeing that the ball was just there for me to basically fall onto or grab a hold of. Again, it was another relief. Some people may call it luck, but I don't really believe that much in good luck and bad luck. I think it's just the way things happen.

Stevie May

It all went as good as we could have ever expected on the day. With their near misses, you just kind of thought it was going to be our day.

Callum Davidson

It happens in games, you see things happen that you can't describe. But I believe if you work hard you get your luck.

Tommy Wright

Why do things not happen? It's crazy. But I always believe. Vincent Lombardi was an American football coach and I put a lot of his signs up, but not all the time. I put them up in the dressing room at times – and I put them up in the cup final. My favourite is 'the harder you work, the harder it is to surrender.' I believe the harder you work, the more you get out of anything and the more you get out of life. And you get those wee breaks in games. How the Ciftci free-kick stayed out... but in any sport there is good fortune. So, maybe, it was in the stars that we were going to win it.

Dave Mackay

When things like the free-kick off the bar happen, you just think it's going to be your day. You certainly do have some games where things go for you and things go against you. You just have that feeling it's going to be your day when things go against the other team.

James Dunne

To be fair, we had a bit of luck in the final. The one off the post in the first half from Dow was literally a centimetre from hitting Alan's back and, in the second half, the Ciftci free-kick came down off the bar literally into Alan's arms. From then, I kind of knew it was our day, being 1-0 up as well at the time.

Steven MacLean

I thought the free-kick was going in, but Alan just sort of sat on the ball in the end. Was it meant to be for us? Maybe it was.

Patrick Cregg

It was just those small margins, everything went in our favour. We carried good bits of fortune throughout the cup run, but you have to – that's football. You can't do well without a bit of good fortune along the way.

> 52 mins 'Wotherspoon to float it in... towards Frazer Wright, nobody on him... and Stevie May scores...! Or has the handball been given here? It's not a goal.' (*Sky Sports*)

Stevie May

It was more just a reaction. I didn't move my hand towards the ball to try and punch it in. The ball was there and I just hit it with my hand – it wasn't intentional or anything like that. I thought it might have already been in the net, but I wasn't sure.

Tommy Wright

I thought it was a goal. Looking back, Stevie didn't try to cheat. I genuinely think he thought the ball had crossed the line. When you look back at it, he was just slapping down on the ball, but it hadn't crossed the line. Without the behind-the-goal-assistant (Alan Muir), the 'goal' might have stood because the linesman was further away. But then the official behind the goal helped us, because he was in a better position to see that there is no way it was a foul on the goalkeeper for our second goal, even though he rolled about after the challenge from 'Macca'. So it was good that we had those officials in the final, and the semi-final as well.

Alan Mannus

I don't remember them having any real opportunities, apart from the one that hit the post in the first half, and the free-kick off the bar in the second half. I think I only had one save to make from Robertson. That was the only save I really had in the game, which showed you how good the defenders were and the guys in front of them. When you look over the course of the five rounds of the cup, we only conceded two goals. That is excellent and shows you how well we defended. 'Ando' and Frazer just won everything in the final and didn't give Ciftci a clear-cut chance. Together with the other lads, we didn't really give them any opportunities – we were just so on it. We worked on some things coming up to the final, the way we were going to do things whenever certain players got the ball and you can see that in the game – the way certain players moved their position. I think we basically shut them down.

Brian Easton
They didn't have a real spell in our penalty area – we were right on the money all day.

Steven Anderson
Ciftci is a quality player. But I think if things don't go his way, he gets a bit annoyed.

Frazer Wright
Ciftci is probably one of their best players. Any advantage you can get, you need to take it. When he is hot-headed, he can go off his game a bit. It was just verbals during the game (to him). He gives as good as he gets.

Brian Easton
You get that in every game – boys winding each other up.

Chris Millar
All the boys were fantastic. I think it's one of the best games I've

seen Frazer Wright play. He had Ciftci in his back pocket, just winding him up the whole game. He was in his ear constantly.

Tommy Wright
We spoke to our two centre halves about dealing with Ciftci, about getting involved if they could with a few verbals with him, but not to get involved, if you know what I mean. He is temperamental. He is such a good player, so we said use any way you can within the rules of the game to upset him, to annoy him. They played him magnificently, the two of them, marked him out of the game.

> 61 mins 'Now Wotherspoon... with Dundee United racing to get back... David Wotherpoon... James Dunne making a run... Wotherspoon is going it alone! Cierzniak makes the save as glory beckoned.' (*Sky Sports*)

David Wotherspoon
'Macca' made a great run to give me an option... Robertson then went that way and slipped and fell over... then I beat (Sean) Dillon and then... I just... hit it straight at him! My head went down and I thought 'right, hit across the goalie' and I hit it straight at him. I think it was just a rush of blood, maybe tiredness, a wee bit of excitement, especially with our fans behind the goal.

Tommy Wright
The second half was cracking for the fans, with Ciftci's free-kick and the controversy of Stevie's disallowed goal. To me the final was epitomised when we defended a corner and David then went on that run, and would probably have scored the greatest cup final goal ever. They then reacted and went up the pitch and Alan pulled off a great save from Andy Robertson, turning his shot around the post.

Chris Iwelumo

Even though I didn't play a part, it honestly felt like I had played in the match. You were so physically drained, it was so overwhelming. We kicked every ball on the touchline.

Michael O'Halloran

The gaffer changed the formation again during the second half, because I went to the right and Stevie May dropped into the left.

Chris Millar

Moving Stevie to the left gave us a little bit more protection. I think all over the pitch we won individual battles.

Michael O'Halloran

Adrenaline took over in the second half. You put a shift in for the team as it was a great chance to win the cup. I knew I was probably coming off for Croft at some point anyway...!

Lee Croft

It was good to come off the bench and get 20 minutes. But it's not nice when you are 1-0 up because you want to make sure you're not the one who comes on and makes a mistake. It was still quite tight at that point. Especially coming on against Robertson, he is quite an attacking full-back so I knew I'd have to do quite a bit of defensive work. I just wanted to do everything right. It was great, a brilliant atmosphere.

> 84 mins 'Stevie May... oh, it's come through to MacLean... he has scored! Steven MacLean! And St Johnstone are staring at the Scottish Cup now' (*Sky Sports*)

Stevie May

The plan, if we needed to, was to change the formation, to change the game. The second goal came from that switch over in the semi-final, when 'Macca' laid it off to me, so obviously it worked. It gives you more defensive cover as well, with pretty much one up front and the five in midfield. We did the same in the final. When we got the second goal, we just had the feeling that was it, then.

Scott Brown
United were looking for the equaliser when 'Macca' scored the second. We were jumping around as much as the supporters.

Chris Millar
I was just so happy for 'Macca'. It kind of typified what he is all about. I knocked it wide to Stevie with a wee header, he drove in, his pass took a wee ricochet off John Rankin, and 'Macca' was in to contest a 50-50 ball. He was always going to win that, that's the type of guy he is.

Gary McDonald
'Macca' likes a tackle and after the ball broke I knew in a 50-50 he was going to win it. At 2-0, I couldn't see them coming back at that time in the game.

David Wotherspoon
It just broke nicely for him, to put it in when he was on the ground. We were always looking to score the next goal so we could just put it to bed. 'Macca' just went mental with his celebration.

Steven MacLean
The goal was the best moment of my career, by a long shot. I've obviously seen the goal back, although I don't really watch games back. It just sort of ricocheted to me. Before the game, the gaffer was saying that their back four don't always keep a good line, as Gunning can jump out and Dillon can be a bit deeper. When you see the goal, that's what happened. The ball just broke to me. I

was hoping to get there a bit quicker and maybe dink it over the goalie, but it ends up a 50-50 and I just tried to take everything to try and put it in the net. Obviously, it's just sort of broken to me and I've been aware enough to just kick it in the net. The rest is history. Without the assistant behind the goal, the referee, Craig Thomson, could have maybe given a foul, but it's after the ball breaks and I kick it in that the goalie starts rolling about. I think he knows himself it's not a foul. Without that assistant, the referee may have given the May handball. Looking at it, the officials had a good game.

Steven Anderson

The keeper rolled around. He came out in the papers saying 'Macca' could have broken his leg. It was a 50-50. It was a fair challenge.

Brian Easton

All credit to 'Macca', he went in not worrying about what would happen to him.

Frazer Wright

When the ball broke, the goalie went for the ball. He was trying to get it and 'Macca' got there first. As soon as it went in the net, that's when he was rolling around.

Callum Davidson

If there was one person in the team you wanted the ball to come to for a 50-50 like that, it was probably 'Macca'. You can see with his reaction to the goal what it meant to him, the top off and going wild. I was absolutely delighted for him. Stevie May got all the plaudits for the semi-final win, and my man-of-the-match was Steven MacLean. He gave us a platform in that game, and he controlled his temperament. And for 'Macca' then to score the late goal in the final, along with the header from 'Ando', was brilliant. Mind you, he could probably do with working on his celebration a little bit, but I'm sure he can't remember what happened!

Steven MacLean

I had a lot of friends and family at the game from Peebles. My wife and my dad were in the hospitality area in the main stand, but my wee boy and the rest of my family and all my mates were in that far corner. I don't know why I took my top off – still don't know why I did it! But I ended up celebrating over in that far left corner and that was it. I didn't see anyone I knew when I was celebrating, but you could smell the alcohol off everybody!

'Mayso' said to me after the game that I had shoved him away when I was celebrating, but I have no recollection of that whatsoever! I can't remember that. I couldn't even remember after the game how the ball had come to me, who had passed it or what. There were only six minutes or so to go, so you know when it's that late on that it would take something monumental from them to get back into it – there was probably no coming back. You knew that it was over, really, so I think that was part of my celebration as well.

Stevie May

I should have just let him get on with celebrating himself! It was a great feeling. It felt as good as scoring a goal yourself when the second goal went in, especially at that stage of the game. If we hadn't got it, it would have been a really nervy last 10 minutes. I was delighted for 'Macca'. But I couldn't have cared if it was an own goal, as long as we had scored. In a final, you just want to get over the line and get the win.

Tommy Wright

When the first goal went in, I didn't realise the United fans were there next to me (on his left) when I was celebrating, pumping my fists. Then, for the second goal, I went on a bit of a run! I had started to put the weight back on (after his operation), so I was bouncing about. It was slippy with the brogue shoes on as well, so I'm lucky I didn't land on my backside. Even though I had realised in the first half that the United fans were in the stand beside me, I started running to celebrate... soon noticing there were no Saints fans in that area. So I had to stop and come back!

Callum Davidson

Tommy keeps telling me how he sped away from me at the second goal, saying I couldn't catch him! It's a story I never hear the end of! But one of us had to be cool on the sidelines, keeping our thoughts focused while he was tearing up and down the pitch side. I'm sure his stitches split at that point and his wife, Anne, was having panic attacks up in the directors' box. It's the quickest I've seen him move! He just took off past me, says I couldn't get near him!

Gary McDonald

I was just about to come on as a substitute and I remember the gaffer absolutely legged it, right in front of the United fans in the main stand after the second goal. I don't know who he was running to! He virtually did the same for the first goal as well. I was thinking 'am I going to have to sit back down again', but thankfully he said 'you're on Gary, just enjoy it, you deserve it'.

Brian Easton

A few minutes after the second goal, I thought 'we've done this'.

James Dunne

When 'Macca' scored the second goal, we were all buzzing. We had that little bit of luck on the day, sometimes you need that, and we were on our way to winning the cup. It was unbelievable.

David Wotherspoon

They tried to put late pressure on, but their chances weren't clear cut. I think we felt comfortable.

Gary McDonald

Coming off the bench, it felt like the pressure was off. It was an enjoyable seven or eight minutes, quite relaxing. It was a question of seeing it out.

Callum Davidson

We had an experienced team, with some good youngsters like O'Halloran, Wotherspoon and May – sometimes that mix allows you to win a trophy. And Dunne, he is a fantastic lad. I would say he is probably not the greatest trainer I've ever seen, but when it comes to games he covers the ground. He plays the game the right way as a central midfielder, he gets up and down, makes a pass, drives the ball, does all the things an overall central midfielder should. He fitted into our jigsaw perfectly. He allowed Chris Millar to go and play as well. Coming up here at his stage in his career from Stevenage, he was down in the doldrums, and I'm disappointed we couldn't get him back for another season.

James Dunne

Unfortunately, Saints had a few injuries in midfield and I came in and went on to win a medal. It was incredible, really. 'Midge' is a good lad and a good player – it was a joy to play with him. We are kind of similar, the way Chris and I play, and Gary McDonald, really. I love tackling, pressing and passing the ball. It was good to play with 'Midgey', he is a nice lad, but all of them are to be fair.

Chris Millar

I felt that James and I complemented each other really well. Even though he came in during January, he fitted in right away. He was vocal on the park, telling boys what to do and organising. I felt the two of us gelled well. If sometimes he was getting forward, I would sit a bit deeper and vice versa. He was at Arsenal as a kid and he knows the game really well. He is a very good football player. I felt we just really clicked as a partnership and I would have loved to have seen him stay, which I know the club tried to do. I thought he was a great signing for us and obviously a part of the success we had. I thought he had a fantastic game in the cup final – he was unlucky not to score. He is a great lad about the changing room as well, always laughing and joking and getting up to nonsense.

Alan Mannus

If United had scored late on it would have been an edgy finish, but they didn't. They had a header wide from Brian Graham right at the end from a corner, but I only really had that one save from Robertson, with two efforts coming off the woodwork. I thought we were pretty comfortable in the game and it was strange at the end knowing there were only a couple of minutes to go. I was thinking 'if we hold on, we're going to win the cup here, how is that possible?!' It was just an amazing feeling. The best thing was that there were so many of our fans there to celebrate and you could see how much it meant to them. I was just trying to watch what was happening on the pitch rather than soak it up – as if they had got a goal near the end it would have been edgy. I was trying to remain focused and calm, as much as I could.

Tommy Wright

I probably had one regret from the cup final. I don't know why, but I only just started thinking about it at the end of 2014 – only making two substitutions. I could have put someone on. Callum and I were talking about it, and he disagrees with me, saying if we had taken someone off they'd have been upset. But I say they would have got a standing ovation coming off. I could have put Nigel Hasselbaink on, who contributed a lot in the season. I could have put Paddy Cregg on, who contributed a lot. I don't know why I didn't, I don't know. Whether it was being the ultimate professional and keeping a sub up my sleeve, just in case they did fire in two goals and forced extra time. Whether that's the reason, but when I look back, that's the one thing I would have liked to have done, put another person on the pitch. It was the right decision to put Gary McDonald on after thinking his season was over.

Gary Miller

When 'Macca' scored with 10 minutes to go, I was hoping to get off the bench. But, in the end, it turned out not to be. You still enjoy the moment, as I'd played my part and been part of the squad the whole way through. It's still yours to enjoy and obviously it's totally different from the last time when I played in the cup final and lost. You enjoy the occasion even more then, because you know you've been back to win it.

Patrick Cregg

I was fortunate to get a winner's medal, but disappointed not to play in the final. All the lads were thinking 'would there be a third sub?' Tommy's argument is fair enough, you've got to accept that. Obviously, the lads who were the unused subs on the bench were thinking 'throw one of us on'. Obviously, from a selfish point of view, you're hoping it's you, but you can't argue with the assessment from the gaffer. That was my first winner's medal in professional senior football. It is a little bittersweet for me, you do want to play, but it was great to be a part of it. I was fortunate enough to play in one with Falkirk, but unfortunately we lost. Listen, I've got a winner's medal and a runner's up medal so you can't really argue with that. Not many people get to play in a Scottish Cup final, let alone be part of a team that wins one. I'm very fortunate in that sense.

Callum Davidson

Unfortunately, it wasn't a time for being sentimental (third sub). It was time to win.

> 90+3 mins 'That's it, they've done it, they've won it. If you are going to wait 130 years to reach the Scottish Cup final, you've just got to go and win it. This is a football first. There is a new name on the world's oldest national trophy, the name of St Johnstone Football Club' (*Sky Sports*)

Steven Anderson

I had been thinking 'kill the game, do what we do, kill games'. So we saw it out, like we did in the Aberdeen semi-final. At the final whistle, I ran to Dave Mackay. It was mad.

Alan Mannus

The thing I remember about the final whistle was Brian Easton running over to me, jumping on me, smiling and not really knowing what to do. He had such a big happy face on him! I felt privileged that I was the first one he ran over to when the final whistle went. He laughs and says he just didn't know what to do, he was just running around.

Brian Easton

Yeah, I ran off to big Alan and gave him a hug. After a few seconds, I saw a few of the boys shaking the Dundee United players' hands and I did that as well, as they had put in their shift and were obviously gutted. Then the serious hugs started among us and we went away to the fans. It was ridiculously good.

Chris Millar

I think if you go through the whole team, from Alan Mannus right through to Stevie May, I don't think any player could have played any better.

Frazer Wright

It was my 100th game for the club and the gaffer's 50th. There's fate again.

Steven Anderson

My mum celebrated her 50th birthday that day as well!

Dave Mackay

I went over to speak to my family, saw the kids and did some interviews. I was on my way back to the podium to get the trophy and someone from the SFA grabbed me and said 'you need to put this on'. To be honest, I wasn't even thinking about it at the time, didn't ask what it was, and they just strapped this GoPro camera onto me for a different player's perspective. I think the woman said to me 'no swearing'. You're on that much of a high, I just said 'no problem'. Whether I'd do it again, I'm not sure, but at the time I wasn't thinking about it. I was just desperate to get on to the podium and get hold of the trophy. I saw somebody else come and put the trophy on the podium, so I thought that was it – I just had to go up, shake the hands of the people from the SFA, get my medal and then go over and lift it.

So I don't know where this man (Ralph Topping from the sponsors, William Hill) appeared from. He came in from the side. Watching it back on TV, he must have been there to hand me the trophy, but I had my hands on it before he came over! At the time, I wasn't sure what he was saying, as I couldn't hear a thing with the noise, but by the looks of it he was trying to pull it back off me! But he wasn't getting that trophy off me! I had my hands on it and wasn't letting it go. The fans had waited so long for a trophy, so I guess they were letting us suffer a wee bit more pain for another couple of minutes!

James Dunne

You can get Wi-Fi on planes now, so my dad was listening to

the commentary on his holiday. I'm sure he was shouting in the plane when he heard the result.

Lee Croft

When we got the second goal, we could then enjoy it. It's the first thing I've won in my career, so it was a great day and something I'll always remember.

Gary Miller

I'll always cherish the medal. Not many people win the Scottish Cup. It's a difficult one to win, especially when Rangers and Celtic were so dominant when I was growing up through my teenage years. To get into your 20s, to get to a cup final and to win it, it's a massive achievement. It's probably something you won't look back on until further down the line and you actually realise what you have achieved. It'll probably be when I stop playing that I realise it more than now.

Steve Banks

The celebrations probably meant a bit more to me this time, from a purely selfish point of view. The fans of any team love winning the cup, but maybe there was a special edge to it because St Johnstone had never won the cup before in their history, whereas Hearts and Dundee United had. To be part of it was certainly very special – and this time I took a step back from the celebrations, enjoying it with family. Rather than jumping around, I took it all in and soaked it up a bit more, watched the lads' faces and saw them enjoying it. I can understand people saying I'm a lucky so and so who has won these medals by sitting on the bench and doing nothing, although deep down I would like to think I contributed in other ways. I can say I did contribute in a playing sense to this one! There are guys who play their whole career without picking up a medal. I've had three clubs in Scotland and got three winners' medals tucked away. I've been so fortunate.

Patrick Cregg

I spent two years with those players and I was delighted for the lads who did play and got that experience. I'm glad for them. Some of them, probably most of them, will never play in a cup final again at that level in Scotland or England. I would have liked to have come on and played, but I was happy for the boys who were on the pitch and I'm grateful to have been part of that experience.

Murray Davidson

I was delighted for everyone at the club and the boys made us feel part of it afterwards. Again, there were mixed emotions at the final whistle. You are so happy for the lads, the manager, the fans and everyone involved. But you feel you have missed out on something special. I saw the lads on the pitch and congratulated them, but Tam and I cleared off out of the dressing room to let the boys enjoy it. It was the biggest mix of emotions I've ever felt, and probably will ever feel. You know you could have been playing, but you're injured and have been for months. It was their moment and I didn't want to be putting a dampener on it. I just felt it wasn't my place to be there jumping about like a mad thing.

Chris Iwelumo

On the pitch afterwards was a fantastic experience. It's difficult to say how good it felt. I think I've experienced quite a lot of great moments, but it was just such an amazing atmosphere. I had goose bumps. It was simply amazing.

Dave Mackay

I was first, obviously, to lead the team out and lift the trophy, but it honestly wouldn't have mattered if I was first or last to lift the cup, as long as we had our hands on it. It was a great feeling. Being a club legend is not something I've really thought about, it's something the fans think about certainly more than the players. I was the first club captain to lift a major national trophy, but then you could say 'Ando' and 'Macca' did the main part by scoring the goals to actually win it. The manager picked the team and put the team together, so I think we're all a huge part of the overall success – the whole squad used over the campaign, the players, the management team, the coaching staff, the physios, the doctors and all staff at the club. It really is that kind of club where everybody pulls together, we're all part of it and can all take huge credit for winning the trophy.

Tommy Wright
After we had won the cup, getting into Europe again wasn't my first thought. But I knew when we got into the dressing room. That made it three seasons in a row for the club in Europe, a significant achievement in itself.

Callum Davidson
I don't believe in all that fate stuff, I just believe in hard work and you make your own luck. If we hadn't worked as hard in the second half of the semi-final then we wouldn't have been in the final. Then if we hadn't worked as hard in the final as we did then we would never have won the game, regardless of fate or anything. I think we were the slightly better team in the final. There were not many people coming out after the game saying we were lucky to win. Dundee United will probably say they didn't play as well as they could, but I'd say that was down to how we played against them, trying to stop them. You couldn't go toe to toe against United and counter attack and counter attack. They had better players in the counter attacking positions, but we had a team of really hard workers with a little flair in there, too.

Dave Mackay
For any cup win, I suppose you have to have a little bit of luck,

you need a good draw and you need your players to perform in one-off games. If you don't turn up, then you're out of the competition. We needed five good performances and we managed to do that. Obviously, a huge part of that success comes down to the manager as well, picking the right players. I think in the semi-final we changed formation a little bit in the second half, as he felt things weren't going quite right. He moved May out to the left and pushed Wotherspoon in a little bit and it worked a treat. So the management play a huge part during the games as well. They'll say it's all down to the players, but obviously the manager and coaches have a huge say in it as well. Owen Coyle, Derek McInnes and Steve Lomas were obviously good managers at the club too, but they just never quite managed to get us to a final. Derek has obviously gone on to lift the League Cup with Aberdeen. I think you just need that little bit of luck as a team, as well as making good decisions and having your players perform for you on the day.

Chris Millar

One of the things that really stuck with me, almost immediately, was how what we did meant so much to so many other people – family, friends and fans. People were so happy and proud of us. For me, I started playing as a wee boy and those are the kind of days you want to savour. You want to represent Scotland, you want to win Scottish Cups, you want to win leagues, whatever. For a club like St Johnstone, to go and win the Scottish Cup, you know how much it means to you and many other people.

8

PERTH PARTY

We'll always keep that blue flag flying high.

'Fair Maid'
The Shrugs

JUBILATION. UNBRIDLED JOY. Sheer, uncontrollable delight. For everyone present at Celtic Park of a blue and white persuasion, those feelings, those memories will never be forgotten. There were songs, smiles, hugs, kisses... and, of course, the odd tear. Finally the world's oldest trophy was coming to Perth — better late than never as they say. Having become the first club to lift the Scottish Cup in their debut final appearance since Jock Stein's Dunfermline defeated Celtic back in 1961, it was party time for the Perth Saints. Yet still, as the players and management passed the trophy around the Parkhead pitch, belted out the lyrics to Sweet Caroline and When The Saints Go Marching In and took famous photos to show the grandchildren one day, there were moments of utter disbelief. There were almost moments of silence. Had the dream finally become a reality? Some simply had to pinch themselves to believe it...

Steven MacLean

It was weird in the dressing room, at first. We went mad and then there was like a lull for 10 minutes. I can remember saying to myself, 'Wow, we have just won the cup here'. We just sat there taking it in.

Michael O'Halloran

It really was a wee bit surreal.

Gary McDonald

My son, Max, is five-years-old and he constantly brings it up all the time. 'Dad, remember the cup final and being on the pitch?' All the time he talks about it. Even though you're not thinking about it, other people remind you of it as well. I've got a picture at home of Max holding the cup. The canvas is in our utility room, so you see it all the time around the kitchen, it's constant. His wee sister, Millie, aged two, is now pointing at it and asking about the cup final!

Gary Miller

It was surreal, really. Watching the DVD back now, I get goose bumps the whole way. It's like 'wow, what a great achievement and what a day'.

David Wotherspoon

I just went crazy, I just couldn't believe it. I celebrated with the boys and then after that I went looking for my family. I was looking for my young daughter, Mia – she was only a few months old – and my fiancée, Sophie. I wanted to get them on the pitch as you always watch these games and see people win the cup and they bring their families on. It just looks nice and that's what I wanted to do – for my family.

Tommy Wright

I think it was reward for the club at the finish, enjoying the celebrations. Even the amount of tickets we sold was great — people thought we wouldn't sell more than 10,000.

Alan Mannus

The celebrations were brilliant, seeing that whole side of the stadium just blue and seeing what it meant to the supporters, walking round and seeing them celebrating. For me, my mum, Margaret, and dad, David, had come over for the game and my fiancée, Leanne, was also there which was nice. The celebrations were great on the pitch and in the changing room afterwards.

Steve Banks

Alan is a hard grafter and self motivated so that has made my job slightly easier. There is a photo of him celebrating in the dressing room with a protein shake while everyone else is having a drink. That is typical Alan! He got a bit of grief for it but it shows his dedication. I did have one beer myself because it's too late for me to bother with protein drinks. Back in my 20's I'd have had a beer with the best of them, celebrating a win and drowning my sorrows after a defeat. But, as I turned 30, I realised that if I wanted longevity I had to think about what I ate and drank. The game changed too, as people were looking after themselves more and I had to change with the times to extend my career. Even now I have different methods of keeping fit and looking after myself.

James Dunne

It was just damn mental in the changing room, spraying champagne everywhere – it was fantastic.

Chris Millar

It was brilliant to get my kids on the park, Ellie and Sophia, having them there. My wee nephew, Rhys, was on as well. They got on to see all the ticker tape, see all the fans and got involved in all the sing songs, which was great because it's as much for them as it is for yourself. My mum, Geraldine, and dad, Ian, were there too. It had been a bad year for my dad with his depression, so it was a real highlight for him.

Tommy Wright

In sport, you have to play to win – winning is everything. At the end of a cup final week and on the day itself, there is just so much emotion. It's not relief – just sheer joy. It was my best day in sport, without a doubt, and my best year. The year couldn't have gone better. That was my 50th game in charge of Saints in my first season, over 10 months of football. But it was a tough year as well, because Anne's dad, David, had passed away the night after we beat Rosenborg. And my mum was ill as well, she eventually died on 27 July. She was called May. That's bizarre as well, given the May connection. My dad, Jackie, wouldn't come to the final because mum had Alzheimer's and cancer and he wouldn't leave her. We had arranged everything, as my sister-in-law wouldn't have come to the final and she would have looked after mum. We had flights ready to go, flying him in the morning, flying straight after the game, but he wouldn't come.

But I still had probably about 25 people over from home. I don't know if it's ever been done before, but after the final I took the cup to one of the lounges in the main stand where they all were. So they all got their photos taken with the cup, not only them, but everybody who was in there as well. Knowing the club, knowing the chairman and his dad, knowing the supporters, to actually get to see other people enjoying the celebrations meant so much. It was just sheer joy. I got letters before the final like 'I'm not a Saints fan, I don't really follow football but my dad was a Saints fan and he went to games all his life'. There were other messages from people saying they were coming from far and wide. It was almost like a pilgrimage for some people and to finally win it was something that I'll never forget. No matter what I do, if I was to go and win the Champions League with another club, it won't eclipse winning the Scottish Cup with St Johnstone. It couldn't, not for the raw emotion and what it meant to people.

Callum Davidson

That's the first trophy I've won. I haven't got a medal for it, but I've got the memories. My greatest achievement in football before then was Scotland caps, especially the Scotland-England Euro 2000 play-off games and the last match at the old Wembley in 1999. I played in that game and we won 1-0, but lost out 2-1 on aggregate. I've been promoted a few times, but looking back on my career Scotland was the biggest thing without a doubt.

Now, if you asked me the question, 'what is the greatest highlight of your career so far?' there is only one answer. I know I wasn't manager and I wasn't playing, but I was assistant manager and played a massive part in it. Winning the cup is my greatest achievement and I don't think I'll ever beat it. The reason for that is that I grew up at St Johnstone, played for them, became assistant manager and then went on to help them win their first major trophy in 130 years. I don't think I'll go to another club that will be like that. That is why, for me, it will probably always be my greatest achievement. If I win the Scottish Cup with another club, yeah it would be nice, but will it be as good as the first major trophy with St Johnstone? Unless they have never won a trophy, then it probably won't be as good, and probably because it's not my club – it's not St Johnstone.

Alex Cleland

I had been involved in cup runs and won championships, but it was my first experience of it as a coach. The feelings were so different. I was absolutely delighted because it's a part of history, helping win the cup as a coach. It was my third time winning the cup, after doing so as a player with Rangers and Dundee United. I think that's something to be proud of. And I was so delighted because it was the club's first time winning the cup – that made it so special. To see the players' faces when we lifted the cup and the celebrations after it, I'll never forget that. I had won it, and they would ask me what it was like, and I was thinking 'you go and tell me, go and win it'. For the fans as well, to see their faces, for them to experience it, was amazing. It was just as good to win it the third time, but it was more special because I can now say I've been involved in winning it as a coach, which is so different to winning it as a player.

Steven MacLean

All the headlines were about May 17, but in the final we definitely showed how much of a team we are. I also remember Stevie saying to me that I deserved it, which showed the sort of guy he is. He never scored in the final, but he played his part just like everyone else. It wasn't about who scored the goals, as we know what we are at St Johnstone. It had been a team effort to get there, with the goals as well as the clean sheets. We know what we are as a team and we pride ourselves on that, being tough to play against. We know we can do the dirty stuff well, but we're a good side too. We maybe don't get the credit for being a good side, but we know we're hard to play against.

Stevie May

I grew up just outside Perth in Newburgh. Regardless of where you are from, winning anything, not just in football but just in general, shows that you have succeeded, especially when it was such a big achievement – the first team in 130 years at the club to have won a major trophy. In terms of Scottish football, realistically, that's as good as it's going to get. Nobody is probably going to beat Celtic to the league, certainly not until Rangers get back. You would be delighted to win the League Cup, but the Scottish Cup is as good as it gets. For me, it was the icing on the cake at St Johnstone.

Frazer Wright

I think it's been a case of Tommy getting the best out of a good bunch of boys here. He knows how to get us to play the way we need to play, using the players we have.

Steven Anderson

I think a big part of the final win was fate. I played in semi-finals under Owen Coyle and we lost on penalties (to Rangers in the Scottish Cup in 2008). I think that's fate, not going to the final. In 2014, it was our time, long overdue.

Liam Caddis

They are your friends and your team-mates, and to see them win the cup was special. It makes you want to be involved in winning a cup in the future. I was so happy for the boys and they deserved to win it.

Scott Brown

We can put our names to the cup win a wee bit because players like 'Cads' and myself did play in the earlier rounds. You saw what it meant to the players in the dressing room, the chairman and people like Paul Smith at the club.

Tommy Wright

Paul has been a rock for me. He was with me all the way through the cup run and does so much at the club. For a guy who has been at the club over 30 years, the cup win meant so much to him.

Tam Scobbie

It was a bitter-sweet season for me. Picking up the injury put a damper on the full season and missing out on the cup final is something that I'll always regret, not being part of the squad. The boys made me feel very welcome in the celebrations and tried to make us a part of it as much as possible, Murray Davidson and myself, but missing out on a cup final like that was a massive disappointment. It's something we both want to try and do again.

Nigel Hasselbaink

I played for Ajax in my youth and we won the league plenty of times, as well as other competitions, but the Scottish Cup win was my first medal as a professional footballer. When you find out the Scottish Cup is the oldest cup in the whole world, it gives you an extra lift, too. Jimmy (uncle, Floyd Hasselbaink) has won a few medals, but even he told me after the game how pleased he was for me. He sent me text messages, saying 'congratulations, well done on winning the cup', so it was good of him. It was big news for everybody, with St Johnstone winning the Scottish Cup for the first time. Just as it was for everyone who supported us, it was a great feeling for them.

Chris Iwelumo

I had never played in the SPL. I came back for six months and I came away from Scotland with a Scottish Cup winner's medal. It's crazy to think back on that, after I retired near the end of 2014 (after leaving Chester). Players who have played in Scotland their whole career at the top level may never have won it. I've experienced quite a lot, enjoyed five promotions, and came back with a winner's medal from Scotland. It's incredible to think of the experiences I had, and that was down to St Johnstone giving me that opportunity. The cup win with Saints is right up there. Obviously, I never played as much as I wanted to at the club, but I still felt part of it. I think it's about what goes on off the pitch as well which is important, and they were just such a great bunch of characters. That really helped the team succeed.

James Dunne

It was nice to get through to a final and, obviously, even better to win it – for everyone at the club. I was also able to win my first trophy. From starting the season and not even playing to ending it playing in the Scottish Cup final and winning it – it was superb. I had won nothing before, only when I was young when we played Sunday League! I won the Sunday League with a team called Orchard, a little local team where I played with all my mates in Kent. In the leagues and the tournaments, we were one of the best teams around in Bromley and Beckenham. When I was at Arsenal as a kid, we lost in the semi-finals of the Youth Cup and I think we finished second in the league, so didn't win anything.

Dave Mackay

It's strange. I've actually never watched the whole final back, although I've seen the highlights a few times. On the day of the game, my Sky box decided to pack in so I couldn't record the game. I had set it to record, got back home and saw that it had failed. I managed to get a DVD from the BBC just before the club brought out their own one, but I've not actually managed to sit down and watch it all and take the whole thing in.

It was 15th time lucky for 'Cup Tie Mackay' to win the Scottish Cup! The nickname finally came good! I've had it since I was in the youth team at Dundee. Jimmy Bone, who was the assistant at the time, gave me it – I assume because it rhymed with Mackay. I never asked any questions of Jimmy, who wasn't the kind of guy you wanted to mess with as a young boy! So it's stuck ever since. I managed to get rid of it when I was down south at Oxford, but it stuck again when I came back up to Scotland. It doesn't bother me at all – in football it's what people know me as.

As the Saints players partied in the dressing room and prepared for a boisterous bus journey back to McDiarmid Park with the famous silverware, there was, however, temporary disappointment for two midfielders...

Chris Millar

After all the celebrations on the pitch calmed down, we headed back in and David Wotherspoon and I got pulled in for the pee test! I was ready to kick on and celebrate, get the drinks flowing, as there was a crateful of beer! But peeing after a game is an absolute nightmare, as it takes ages. Once you pee you can go away and come back, but you can't go until you do your first bit.

David Wotherspoon

We went into the tunnel, ready to celebrate with the boys in the dressing room, and they pulled 'Midge' and me aside and said 'drug test'. It was the biggest disappointment of the cup final, having to go and do a drugs test, where you sit in a room and you're not allowed to go unless you, basically, do a pee. The boys were celebrating with champagne and we were there. Rather than go into the dressing room you've got to go straight into a room. They pick out two names. And because you've played you are dehydrated.

Chris Millar

Gavin Gunning and Sean Dillon were there with us from Dundee United, but they were great and were very gracious in defeat, saying we deserved to win and offered their congratulations. I managed to pee a bit to start with but then had to come back to finish off. I had missed all the singing with the champagne, but got in with the boys for a load of pictures with the cup in the dressing room. You want your memories. I felt a wee bit sorry for David, celebrating himself, but I managed to get involved with the lads a wee bit, although I was one of the last players on the bus.

David Wotherspoon

I basically couldn't do it – it took me at least half-an-hour to 45 minutes to do anything. Eventually I managed to get something out and I went to the dressing room and nobody was there, everyone was gone. All the gear was gone, so I basically missed out on all the memorabilia, apart from the stuff that I had in my cupboard, which was my strip. I just thought it was very disappointing, I was quite angry at the time. It's my only bad memory about it. Apart from that, it was an unbelievable day and weekend. Everyone was just buzzing. It was fantastic.

Gary McDonald
Fair enough, I think the test is fine after the end of a league game. But I think after a cup final it needs looked at.

Lee Croft
It was a great journey back to the ground – we were taking loads of photos and selfies with the cup. I remember May and I poured all our beer into the cup and then the chairman wanted the cup down the front... but it was full of beer at the back!

Chris Millar
The bus was brilliant. We were dancing, drinking, taking photos on our phones and the boys were up singing on the microphone. I was up doing that, as I think of myself as a bit of a singer, going back to my schooldays and our wee boy band! I'm partial to a bit of karaoke. We were filling the cup up with beer and everybody got a swig out of it. It was just brilliant. I was pretty drunk by the time we got off the bus at Perth!

Nigel Hasselbaink
Everyone was in great spirits on the bus back to Perth and I was looking forward to seeing family and friends who had come over from Amsterdam.

It was an amazing night for Saints and for the city of Perth, as frenzied celebrations were enjoyed into the early hours. And the pubs didn't do too badly either...

Tommy Wright
It was a great night. The ground was going mad, all the bars were busy. Players, wives, friends and people who work at the club

were all enjoying themselves. We had a bit of a party in my office and some of the players came down for a drink. The celebrations were good.

Dave Mackay

The celebrations were fantastic, coming back to the stadium on the Saturday night. You are on such high on the bus on the way back and then you see your family at the stadium and have a wee chat. Then you have a little bit of come down. We were just sitting have a drink, and about four or five of the players ended up in the manager's office downstairs, while others were mingling about upstairs with family.

Tommy Wright

I was back to being the 'Ballyclare Barman' in my office that night! My desk had turned into a bar. It was very slick service!

Frazer Wright

I think I was drunk when we got to the stadium! It was a brilliant night. I had the kids, the whole weekend they were there, so that was great. I think there was karaoke in the Muirton Suite. I think...

Stevie May

I can't remember too much about the Saturday celebrations!

Murray Davidson

We had a great night. It was good to be part of it. In a way, it was quite subdued on the Saturday night compared to the Sunday, probably because the lads were tired after all they had put into the game. But it was great to be part of the celebrations.

Steven MacLean

It was a great night on the Saturday, to make so many people happy and have all the family there. It was a big celebration up in Perth and on the bus on the way back up – it was fantastic. All my family were in Perth, it was great to spend it with them and get pictures with the cup. A few of the boys then went out into town.

For some, the city centre nightspot, the Loft, was the favoured choice on a night to remember... or try to remember...

Brian Easton
I was in the Loft with a good few of the boys – Croft, Dunne, Miller and O'Halloran. I remember the music went off and the lights came on at the end, about 3am, but nobody really left, everyone was jumping about singing St Johnstone songs. I looked over and saw Mikey on people's shoulders, the fans throwing him about. It was quality. I think I was still drunk the next day...

Michael O'Halloran
I was just dancing and some guy just put me up on his shoulders. Gary Miller was up as well, and we were just bouncing! It was good fun.

Lee Croft
You couldn't move. It was crazy. I remember being at the top area and the whole dance floor was singing songs up to us. I felt like I was in the Beatles.

Gary Miller
People were just grabbing us onto their shoulders and jumping about! The lights came up and the jumping about delayed everybody getting out. They were holding us up, so it was all a bit surreal. It was a bit mental – it was like we were kings. But everybody was enjoying it – everybody was delighted for us and obviously delighted to be St Johnstone fans.

It was just a great atmosphere the whole day, the game and at night back up in Perth. I'll always remember those moments. Football is a hard game for players at times, but to lift a cup and then to celebrate it with the fans is something that you don't often get in Perth. For the lads, it was a brilliant experience. The boys have spoken about it since then and it's a great memory for us all to have. Something like that doesn't come about very often, so for us it was surreal, really.

Tommy Wright

I watched the game again about 3am in the morning. I've got it stored on the memory, Sky and BBC. In the BBC coverage, you saw how much it meant to people like Allan Preston and he spoke very well. On Sky, my best mate Michael O'Neill was chuffed to bits. The club's DVD then came out and the memories are nice. I think I've watched it once since then and still get goose bumps. Gordon Strachan rang me the morning after the final, and it was the first time I'd ever spoken to him. I thought it was nice of him to congratulate me, but I didn't want to say I was rushing to get ready for the bus parade and I was running late! He just went through my team and said how well they had done. He said how proud I must be – and that was nice for him to take the time. I had other messages. I'm close friends with Neil Lennon and I know Ally McCoist well, and they both contacted me. Then there were people that I've played with and mates, like Barry Hunter, the chief scout at Liverpool. People were just so pleased. I received nice club letters from Newcastle and Manchester City, too. Loads of people got in contact and I think there was genuine pleasure for St Johnstone winning it, not only from people I know but throughout the country. Even in the build up to it, I think people genuinely wanted us to win because we hadn't won it before.

Chris Millar

Saturday night in Perth is a bit of a blur! I do remember the next morning, getting into the club and Roddy Grant called me into his office. It was about mid-morning and he pulled a bottle of champagne out of his drawer, cracked it open and Roddy and I sat in and drank it before we went on the open top bus!

Nobody could have predicted the Sunday scenes in the Fair City. More than 25,000 supporters packed the streets as an open-topped bus made its way from McDiarmid Park to the central, packed Horsecross Plaza, just outside Perth Concert Hall. People with scarves, flags and jester hats simply painted the town blue, while the famous trophy glistened in the sunlight. There were photographs aplenty, a pipe band, a replay of the final on a big screen and a stage to welcome the team. It was a day like no other. An afternoon that made a mockery of claims that Perth is not a football city. Men, women, girls and boys – to a person they simply had a ball as the club's new heroes basked in the adulation.

Dave Mackay

The Sunday was fantastic for everybody involved. We just never expected anything like the scenes we saw in Perth, with the amount of people that turned out. On the bus, just leaving the stadium, among the boys you're thinking,' is there going to be a couple of thousand or whatever dotted about the streets?' But to drive through the streets and then to get into Perth centre was amazing. Coming into the area at Perth Concert Hall, seeing the numbers, it was absolutely incredible. It just made the day so special, especially for people with kids to have them there. It's a day they will never forget.

I guess it was an outpouring of emotion after everything – the build up, the fact the club had never won anything before and people saying we could never get over the final hurdle. We had managed to do it in a semi, but could we do it in a final? And everyone was still tipping Dundee United despite our results against them. I think that helped as well, that people were kind of writing us off a little. It was just a feeling of relief, seeing the joy on the fans' faces after the game and, obviously, the Sunday as well. It was just sheer delight from people. They maybe don't all turn up every week at games for whatever reason – families, money issues and things like that – but they made sure they were part of that occasion in Perthshire. I'm sure there were people who turned up who weren't even Saints fans, just to see it, to be a part of it.

My daughter, Louise, loved all the attention on the Sunday. She turned 12 that day and she was up on the stage, people singing happy birthday to her. It's something that she will never forget, as well. My young boy, Callum, was almost 11 months at the time, so he won't remember much about it – he'll have to see it on TV. But for someone my daughter's age, I'd imagine it is something that will stick with her for the rest of her life.

Gary Miller

Going through the streets, we couldn't believe how many fans were actually out. We didn't think it would maybe last that long, but I think we were on the bus 45 minutes to an hour. Then we arrived in the centre and I don't think any of the lads could believe it – thousands and thousands of people everywhere! The bus was even struggling to get through. The lads were just a bit taken aback, it reinforced what it meant to everybody and how big an achievement it was. Obviously we had realised, but when you see a scene like that it's a bit special – this is something different. I can remember a lot of the lads trying to take pictures on their phones. They were never really able to take it in at the time, so they were trying to capture a bit for themselves. It was terrific.

Steven Anderson

What epitomised the achievement for me was the Sunday, the

reaction. Saturday night was fairly quiet for me, as I went back down the road as my wife, Sarah, was pregnant. But the Sunday made up for it.

Frazer Wright
Around about the streets on the bus tour it was busy, but it wasn't too busy. Then when we got into the town it was mental. It was great.

James Dunne
The number of fans who turned up was unbelievable. The whole town was rammed. I was at the front of the bus singing, but I was a bit worse for wear by then after too many drinks!

David Wotherspoon
I expected some crowds, but I didn't expect that. We saw people around the streets, everyone coming out of their houses, and when we got into the centre, along the High Street and then turning the corner, it was just floods of people. I was right at the front of the bus the whole time, I didn't move! I had the cup as well!

Lee Croft
I was at the front of the bus too, with Scobbie and May. It was a brilliant day. It just makes you want to do it all again, I'd love to do that. Once you've had a taste of something like that, you just want it again.

Michael O'Halloran
Sometimes you find yourself just sitting thinking about it and it does give you that determination to try and go and replicate it.

Chris Millar
I kept being told to be quiet on the bus because I was too loud!

Tam Scobbie

I can't remember much about the Sunday on the bus! It was a great day. Saturday night was good as well, we had our families at the stadium, and then Sunday was obviously the parade. The fans were excellent. The bus journey was a real highlight of the whole weekend for a lot of the boys, to see so many fans. It was just great to be a part of it.

Stevie May

On the Sunday I couldn't do too much, as on the Monday morning I had a 7am drive to Largs for Scotland Under-21 duty. I had to watch what I was doing, unfortunately!

Callum Davidson

You don't know how many people are going to be out for a bus tour. So it was great to see people out waving and I was thinking 'this is a nice little jaunt through Perth'. I was born in Stirling, but my grandfather lived in Perth so I knew a few faces. Then as we turned into the High Street it was just like, 'wow'. The things that live with me are the 15,000 St Johnstone fans at the game, then on the Sunday my two daughters were on the bus with me, Carrie and Eilidh. Going up that street and just seeing them all, round the corner to the Concert Hall, it was amazing, absolutely amazing. I didn't realise there would be so many people. It was just great to see everybody out, all the blue and white. It was a real celebratory experience, and it was good that it was done on the Sunday. It was funny, after it all calmed down later in the afternoon, my family and I all walked into a cafe and everyone stood up and clapped. It was really nice and my kids were absolutely buzzing.

Nigel Hasselbaink

It was unbelievable, seeing all the supporters in Perth. It was simply all blue. It was a great feeling to see how many people came out and gathered in the centre, to celebrate with us. Being on that bus tour, we saw how happy everyone was and how happy they were for us. I was glad to see all the supporters happy, and the boys, and all the directors. Those are memories that will stay with me forever, 100 per cent. It's one of the best feelings.

Chris Millar

It was unbelievable. There was just a real carnival atmosphere about Perth. It was brilliant. It just showed you how many people it touched and how they felt part of it, sharing in our success. For me, that was one of the highlights. I gave my medal to fans to wear to get pictures taken. It was just an amazing atmosphere. It meant so much to people to wear the medal, so it was great to share it with them, to see how the cup win affected so many.

Gary Miller

Coming off the bus, we then had to walk through onto the stage that was set up for us, where (writer, broadcaster and Saints fan) Stuart Cosgrove was compère. Again, it was a bit crazy – you realised how many people were there. It was just great to enjoy the moments.

Steven Anderson

With Stuart introducing us on stage to the fans, it was fantastic.

Tommy Wright

After the parade, we had the Player of the Year Awards at the club on the Sunday night. I had a speech to make, so it was a long day. I was absolutely knackered come 9pm. The chairman called me 'weak' because there was still a disco on, but I couldn't physically keep my eyes open.

Chris Millar

After the Awards, I think I was the last player in the Loft. I was in the DJ booth that night, I remember that. It must have been about 1am and I just hit a brick wall. I knew I had to get myself away for a sleep.

During times of success, there are moments of quiet contemplation. As the reality of what they had achieved began to sink in, the Saints players knew such a high simply had to be savoured given many had endured tough times before.

Steven MacLean

You look back at times when you were injured, and that's why you work so hard to get back for moments like the cup final success. You go through bad spells when you are injured and you think 'why do I do it?' but the cup win was a reason why. It's why you make so many sacrifices in your career for moments like that.

Steven Anderson

Every year you think back to where we have come from, what we have achieved, as every year recently, since we came back to the top flight, we have kind of progressed. Look at the days when we were third bottom of the First Division and we were struggling. It was massive for us to win the First Division in 2009 having been in that league for so long. I remember in 2007 when we just missed out on promotion to Gretna, after that day at Hamilton. We thought we had done it after winning there, but it was a late kick-off at Ross County and James Grady scored late on for Gretna. We were in the dressing room waiting for the final score and Stevie Milne was listening on the radio. His face said it all. Now we're an established top-flight team and, obviously, we have now won something.

Frazer Wright

I joined Stranraer in the First Division, got relegated to the Third

Division and then helped them get back to the First Division – and then left. I was a car mechanic at the end of that spell, while I also worked in Dixons. You definitely think back to where you were. I put in a lot of hard work over the years to get here, and you do think about it. I used to go to work, go to training and then play. Now, this isn't really a job for me, I go and play football. But I'm going to have to get a normal job soon, so I'm trying to make it last as long as I can.

Brian Easton

I got injured at Dundee in season 2012-13, came back and then we got relegated, so it wasn't a very a good season. But I did well in the second half of the season and the Saints gaffer at the time, Steve Lomas, liked me before I signed for Tommy. Coming here, it's been really different to that season at Dundee.

Alan Mannus

For me, the best thing about it all was that I was able to be part of the squad that brought the trophy to the club. St Johnstone gave me my chance to come over here, and have been brilliant to me, but to be part of the squad who won the trophy for the supporters, who had wanted it for so long and it meant so much to, was amazing. They have all been unbelievable to me and I couldn't have asked for people to have treated me any better. Before I got my chance playing, they were saying nice things to me and have sung my name. I never expected to get treated as well as I have been. So for me to help give them that day, and that season, then I'm thankful to have been a part of that. How else can you repay people who have been so good to you? I also think a big part of our success over the season was the dressing room. There is a great bond between the players. It's something that can really help you out.

Stevie May

You can always be optimistic going into a season, but 27 goals, a

Scottish Cup winner's medal and then, later, a full Scotland cap – you would have been called 'cocky' if you had predicted that! Tommy probably gave me my second chance, because my first chance was getting my debut and playing a lot of games under Derek McInnes, before I went out on loan. But Tommy gave me that chance after being out on loan to come and play in the first team again, taste European football, and thankfully it was a successful season. I was able to repay him. I've obviously still got a lot of friends at the club, so I definitely keep an eye on how Saints are doing from down at Sheffield Wednesday.

Tommy Wright

Stevie's goals got highlighted, but Stevie never thought of himself as the star of the team, other people did. But Stevie was like the Christmas tree with the star on the top, or like your cake, with your finishing on the top. He was that special piece, but he is a piece. It can be summed up that we won the cup without him scoring – that reflects our team ethos. Stevie knew the number of assists David Wotherspoon, for example, had throughout the season. That's why Stevie gets his success, I believe. He is well grounded, like most of them are, and he knows the importance of the team. It's not about him – it's about the squad and the team.

Steven Anderson

May scored goals and, if you do well as a striker, you get a move – simple as that.

Patrick Cregg

The May 17 final date and Stevie's shirt number was an amazing coincidence, wasn't it? It's incredible the way it worked out. I know we were fortunate with the draw up to the semi-final, but we took advantage of it, and that's the main thing. It'll be hard for the club to do anything like that again.

Sanel Jahic

It was a big trophy for St Johnstone to win, it was their target, to go and win a trophy. It's not easy to be league champions in Scotland for a club like them and the Scottish Cup was a good possibility to pick up a trophy.

Lee Croft

I was on Soccer Am on Sky Sports the week after the cup win. They asked me to go down with the medal. They were laughing, said the medal was tiny! They did a few things before the final with 'Mayso' and I, and we sent a few videos in and a few pictures and stuff. I know a few of them at Sky as I used to do 'Lee Croft Storyteller'. It was good that they showed an interest in us, and the lads enjoyed it.

Tommy Wright

I look at the improvement since Steve Lomas and I came in to the club, some made under Steve, some since I took charge, and it pleases me. We now have a full-time physio for the Under-20s, a full-time sports scientist, a grass training surface at the back of the stadium that is improving all the time, a modern astro pitch and we've made other improvements to the gym. It takes time and I'm comfortable with that, because I understand the club can't commit a massive outlay in one season to do things. So we do things in stages. The biggest thing, as well, particularly over the last 12 – 18 months, has been working closely with Alistair (Stevenson) to improve the underage levels. Alistair, Alex, Callum and I are all part of the team trying to bring young players through. Alistair knows that if he brings through a 17 or 18-year-old I'll put him on the pitch, which I think is important. On and off the pitch, things are happening and we're building blocks to make the club better all the time. We just get on with it quietly, which is how the club likes to do things.

For some players, however, it was the end of the road. After the weekend celebrations, Monday proved a difficult day for Wright and those being released.

Tommy Wright

I was brought back down to earth going back into work on the Monday, as I had to bring in people like Paddy Cregg and release him. Nigel Hasselbaink had gone, he made a decision to go even though it would have been nice to sit down with him face-to-face and thank him. Big Chris Iwelumo knew he was getting released, but 'Padge' probably didn't and that was tough. But I gave him an honest answer and told him I needed to bring the younger players through, like Scott Brown. That's my point about life, you just have to get on with things – whatever is going to be is going to be. You have to deal with things as they come your way because life goes on. That's the attitude I take with things, but it wasn't nice, I must say, it wasn't nice.

Patrick Cregg

It was definitely a tough day for me, but that's the way it goes. I didn't really know which way it was going to go, but there wasn't anything there for me. I had to take it on the chin and move on.

Nigel Hasselbaink

I had two great seasons at the club, played in the Europa League, won the Scottish Cup and everyone was good – the players, the manager, the chairman. I liked staying in Perth, but I just wanted a new challenge at that time. Winning the cup was a great note to leave on.

Chris Iwelumo

You kind of know if you are staying or not, and I probably didn't play as much as I wanted. But the first thing Tommy said to me in that meeting was 'if I had to sign you again, I would'. He knew what I had brought, what I did on the pitch, as well as what I did off it. I think that's testament to the man himself. Football is football. It was a tough one for 'Padge', he was in just before me. When I signed for Chester, people were saying I should have just checked out with the Scottish Cup winner's medal, but I kind of did. It's not been a bad way to finish up my career.

Indeed, for all involved in St Johnstone's greatest-ever triumph, 17 May 2014 will simply never be erased from memory banks.

Stevie May

The cup final win is something nobody can ever take away from us. It's something we can always look back on. We've got the medal, you can always look back online to see pictures of the day – we will always have that success. It's obviously something to look back on proudly. I'll definitely be showing all the photos to the grandkids one day, hopefully.

David Wotherspoon

My move (from Hibs) worked out brilliantly, I couldn't have asked for a better season. It felt unbelievable. Growing up being a Saints fan, I had been to the semi-final when they lost to Rangers at Hampden (in 2008). I've been there, I've been disappointed. So to finally do it and actually be playing was just unreal. Having a lot of friends and family supporting the club, it just meant a lot. I'll always remember it.

Steven Anderson

After my career, I'll be able to look back and think I've done something but, at the moment, you still want more. You still want to be successful and achieve more every year.

James Dunne

The cup win with St Johnstone holds massive affection. I looked at it as if I was playing in the English FA Cup, to be honest. To win it, especially because I'd had a bad season up until January when I went on loan to Saints, made the season even better for me. I'll never forget it. Winning the cup increased my profile, but I didn't think moving back to St Johnstone after my loan was good for me, really. For personal reasons, I needed to be near home and Portsmouth came in for me. I went on holiday and rang Tommy when I came back and just explained it to him. He was brilliant. I just thanked him for the chance he had given me – otherwise I could have been sitting in the stand for the rest of the season. He gave me the opportunity to come up and play and I ended up winning a medal. I really enjoyed it up there and I always look out for their results. I still speak to 'Croftie' and a few of the other boys. I'll always want them to do well.

Tommy Wright

We moan when people say we are under the radar, but we quite like it. It means we can get on with our job. They all turned up in that final and that was the case all season. For us to get the two European away wins, top six again, semi-finals of the League Cup and then win the cup, you need more than 11 players for that. 'Macca' is one of the leaders in the dressing room – he's tremendous on and off the field. We have quite a few leaders, from the captain, Dave Mackay, to maybe five or six others.

Dave Mackay

You've got to enjoy the highs, because there are plenty of lows in football. At the level I've played, you probably lose more games than you win over your career. I went through administration at Dundee. I managed to get out of Livingston just before they went into administration again, but the whole year there was an absolute nightmare. After going through times like that, then you obviously savour days like winning the Scottish Cup. I think the older you get as well, you appreciate it more. When you are younger – I played my first cup final with Dundee when I was 23 – you maybe think it will happen all the time. It was my first full season in the first team, playing every week, and you just think 'these things are going to come round so often in your career'. People tell you all the time, 'it's such a short career, enjoy it', but when you're younger you never really listen to that. You think there are 10 to 15 years ahead of you and you'll manage to do this and that. But I think the older you get, you realise finals don't come around very often and you've got to really enjoy them, which I did.

Callum Davidson
I started my career at St Johnstone when I was young, aged 15 or 16, then obviously played for them and moved on, making some money for the club in the process (£1.75m club record transfer fee to Blackburn Rovers). So, for me, to come back and play for Saints again, manage to finish my career with them, then move into my current role has been great. I've been very fortunate to be at the club during some of the most successful times in their history. But I feel like I'm trying to give them something back as well, helping them as much as I can, so it's brilliant. I'm pretty lucky, to be honest.

Tommy Wright
I don't like the word 'legend'. I don't think I'm the greatest manager in the club's history. I've never liked the word 'legend' and I think it's used far too often. It's not being blasé, or anything like that, I just don't like the word. I know Owen and Derek assembled good teams and just came up short in cup competitions, so maybe for me it was just good fortune. I don't know. Maybe, as a group, everything just fell into place at the right time. We had some luck of the draw, but even so, Rangers were beaten at Forfar that season

and Raith beat Hibs in the cup. History will show you St Johnstone have lost away to other so-called smaller clubs, but I think we had a mentality and a belief. We had always instilled in the players that we could beat anybody on any given day – and that was important. It's great to look back at things as you don't always see everything. There is a picture after the semi-final of Wright, Millar, Mackay and Anderson hugging on the pitch and that sort of epitomised it for me. They had gone through heartache, but they had now won a semi-final. They almost realised that their time had come, and it was how they dealt with the final. We wanted them to enjoy the occasion, embrace it, not play the occasion but play the game – and they did. But to win anything you need everybody on that day to give everything, and that's what we had. If you marked our players against every one of their players, our players were all individually better on the day. How you get there, I think, is to instil a belief in them.

Callum Davidson

After it all, I remember Tommy and I said 'where do we go from this?' Expectations rise and budgets are tight and it's difficult to win trophies, especially after you win your first major one after 130 years. But you have to set yourself goals and push on. It's a great feel-good memory to have, but we don't look back, you have to look forward. We've still got a job to do and we want to move forward. But, by the same token, you have to celebrate it, as it took 130 years. It makes you smile every time you think about it – every St Johnstone fan will agree. If you think about the 17th of May you will have a smile on your face. We will do for the rest of our lives.

Tommy Wright

Anne got a bulldog pup in July 2014, he's called Winston. But she found out when we got his papers that he was born on May 17. Did I mention fate?

POSTSCRIPT
BY STEVE BROWN, CHAIRMAN

IT'S ACTUALLY HARD to put into words what it felt like when the final whistle sounded at Celtic Park. For a moment, I actually stood in disbelief – I couldn't believe what I was seeing. I received a text from the Inverness chairman, Kenny Cameron, saying 'smile, you're on the telly'. My mind was saying 'St Johnstone have just won the Scottish Cup. Have we really done it?' It was an incredible feeling. With all our fans at the other side of the stadium, I was actually transfixed watching the supporters enjoying themselves. It was joyous, but I wondered if it was actually just a dream after waiting so long to see it.

Then, coming to the club on the Sunday morning with the trophy, there were people everywhere. You saw what it meant to people. There were people in tears in the car park, the Holy Grail was mentioned and people were saying 'I have to touch it. Can I touch the cup?' People were hugging us all, it was amazing. Then going through the streets on the bus tour and recognising fans and Perth citizens – it was brilliant to see how happy they were that we had won it. It was a very, very emotional day – enjoyable, but emotional. And, of course, you think back to the darker days the club had endured before.

My dad, Geoff, came in essentially to save the club, in 1986, so there are almost 30 years of Brown history here. I started following the club in 1979-80 and it was in 1983 when we won promotion from the First Division after going to Alloa – I remember Andy Brannigan's overhead kick. However, there was soon talk about financial problems at the club and I recall

Steve and Geoff Brown with the Scottish Cup. *Graeme Hart*

standing on the terracing at the old Muirton Park – it was just crumbling. I couldn't believe it when one of my mates told me that my dad, who had followed the club since he was a youngster, had bought St Johnstone! It was a strange feeling. Even at that point, I still didn't appreciate how perilously close the club was to going out of business – it was on the cliff edge. It could have been a case of another Third Lanark.

Since then to the present day, for me it's been a case of a club living within its means finally getting its just rewards. As a supporter and a director, losing the First Division title on the final day to Gretna in 2007 was probably one of the lowest points, it certainly would be in the top five. We won 4-3 at Hamilton, a very tricky game, only for Gretna to score in the 95th minute as we waited on the score – it was just a sickener. Gretna only existed just over a year after that. It didn't matter if they trampled on clubs living within their means on their way up – the media liked the romance of it. They almost won the Scottish Cup. Now they're not here and we are, with a Scottish Cup win to show for it. It's taken a long, long time for our financial policy to kick in, but I'm glad it did in the end. We're proud to say any money we've used is generated by ourselves, and we're proud to say we've won a major national trophy.

Personally, it was a great thrill to see my dad's beaming smile at full-time at Celtic Park. You think about all the grief, all the effort and all the time he put in during those 25 years as chairman, so I was delighted for him. It's been some journey as a family. In between playing football, I came and watched games when McDiarmid Park sprang to life, bringing my two sons, Daryl and Ryan, along. It's probably something I miss more than anything, just being an ordinary punter. We were back on the ascendancy from the late-80s, with the opening of McDiarmid in 1989, sold-out 10,000 crowds and the 5-0 win over Aberdeen in 1990. Things like that never leave you. Daryl was a mascot in the League Cup final against Rangers at Celtic Park in 1998.

He still has the framed signed shirt, taking pride of place in our house.

We went back down to the First Division and it took a number of years to get us back out, thanks to Derek McInnes and his team in 2009. I had been on the board since 2004 and it just seemed the obvious thing for me to take over from my dad. You have almost served your time after seven years on the board and my move was probably triggered by Derek leaving the club. Any change of chairman when a manager is in place is probably not too clever in terms of working continuity. Dad had gone through 25 years and it was a hard, hard stint for him. He probably wanted out before then as it can be a real burden, some days are really thankless, but they are offset by the good times.

But nothing can prepare you for the role of chairman. You do your best and when you make mistakes you just have to learn from them. I was doing interviews for the manager's job before I knew it and Steve Lomas came in, with Tommy as his assistant, who I got to know really well. When Steve left after the success he had with us – back-to-back top sixes and consecutive European campaigns – I had it in my mind what I was looking for and I knew what Tommy could offer us. I was quite comfortable bringing him in as manager.

Tommy knew what we craved. We were the biggest club in Scotland not to have won anything of significance. When you were on the terraces or in the stands, you heard words to that effect and it rankled with us. We didn't seem to get the luck of the draw, get the rub of the green in certain games and we had been to so many semi-finals. Frustration wasn't the word for it. Tommy knew staying up, as ever, was the priority, but winning a cup would be beyond anybody's wildest dreams, more so for the supporters. I remember Tommy looking across the table at me and saying 'I'll win you a cup' – just like that, nonchalant. His belief had a lot to do with us winning the cup, it was unbelievable. I was trying to play it down a bit, taking it a game at a time, so

I was always anxious. Tommy kept saying 'don't worry, relax, our name is on the cup', especially when May 17 came apparent with Stevie May's surname on his shirt and number matching the final date. He said things happen in football, and I guess he was right. There was no stopping them in the end, especially after coming back to beat Aberdeen in the semi-final. All the players got this feeling, not an over-confidence, but there was a mindset, you could feel it, that they were going to do it.

The players were desperate to win it. I could relate to supporters who said just getting to the Scottish Cup final after so many years was a great achievement, but my mind doesn't work like that. If you're in it, you've got to win it. The opportunity was there and we couldn't miss it. We might never ever get another chance, so we had to take it. I didn't sleep the night before the final. I was up walking about in the living room, so nervous. But I knew the camp was so vibrant and high, there was a great atmosphere. I had stayed with the team before the semi-final, but I was committed elsewhere the night before the final, which the manager wasn't too happy with as he wanted everything the same as for the semi. All the directors met in the boardroom on the morning of the game, getting our heathers for our suit lapels, similar to a wedding I suppose. It was very, very quiet, even going down on the bus. I just kept looking out the window, I couldn't really engage with anyone, just had wee conversations. I was trying to dream and it was a great feeling seeing all the Saints buses travelling down.

Roddy Grant was sitting not too far from me in the directors' box at Celtic Park and when Nadir Ciftci's free-kick came down off the underside of the bar, with us then 1-0 up thanks to Steven Anderson's goal, he gave me that look to say 'that's it, we've won it.' I guess you need luck; it's part of the game. Sometimes you get it, sometimes you don't. But I didn't believe Roddy, I was still sitting there pouring with sweat, the nervous tension of it all. Even when we went 2-0 up through Steven MacLean, I still didn't think it was over. I've watched St Johnstone for long enough now to know that we usually sit back and soon concede a goal! But, fair play, to them, they didn't sit back and we saw the game out, as United ran out of ideas.

When the first goal had gone in, we kind of forgot who we were as directors! But I was conscious that we had Dundee United supporters sitting in front of us and we didn't want to upset them. When we scored the second goal, it was crazy, clambering over each other, cheering, it was just the emotion of it all. Some folk might have taken offence at it, but it was the emotion for us. Tommy was away running down the track celebrating anyway! To me, 2-0 was a fair result – I thought we deserved the score. We had proved we were more than capable on any day, but we needed that wee cutting edge during the season and Stevie May provided it. But the squad was a good mix, with different age groups. James Dunne proved to be a great signing in midfield. A lot was made of Stevie's goals, but we had 23 clean sheets during the season to show the importance of the defence.

Coming back on the bus after the final, I thought of the late club legends who would have loved the day – guys like Drew Rutherford and Don McVicar. I guess that's quite morbid after winning a cup, but you think like that. I used to love watching Rutherford slide tackling from 15 yards, while McVicar was hard as nails. There were also people who I knew personally who didn't see the final – my grandad, Charlie, died in February 2013. He went home and away watching Saints. I obviously thought about him, as well as quite a number of other fans who I knew around the club. I also know of supporters who have passed away since the final win, but I'm glad they at least got to see it.

Of course, Sunday in Perth was amazing. It was so emotional. You wonder if fans will come out, but how they did! By the time our whistle stop bus tour got down to Bridgend and Tay Street, it was like ants, there were people everywhere. By the time we reached the pedestrian area, I've never seen so many people in Perth. I didn't know there was that many in Perth, just thousands of people came out. It was a guess to say there were 25,000 people lining the streets. It was great for Perth and the city may never see that again. We would love to see more of the people who supported us in the final, and on those streets, come to McDiarmid Park on a more regular basis.

In my opinion, Tommy Wright is the finest manager the club has ever had – not just because he delivered a trophy but his overall performance to date. Alex Totten was here quite a number of years and the success he enjoyed was primarily taking us through the leagues and into the Premier Division. Willie Ormond was good enough to leave us, after taking the club into Europe for the first time, and become the Scotland manager. But they didn't win the Scottish Cup. Tommy is always very modest and he wants to be judged on the longevity of his reign, but encompassing everything he has already done – winning away in Europe twice, achieving the top six last season, getting to the semi-final of the League Cup and winning the Scottish Cup, nobody in St Johnstone's history has achieved that lot.

The targets we set are still high here, but sometimes great plans don't come to fruition. The biggest thing we have to manage now is the expectation levels. We have made a rod for our own backs. Since Derek McInnes brought the team back up in 2009, the last six years have been very good for the club. We just want to keep trying to improve, to be as successful as we possibly can. We genuinely thought we had a real chance of retaining the cup in 2015, so that was disappointing – but there are a lot of good football teams out there. The philosophy within the club is to win as many games as we can, and if we win another trophy then even better. We'd love to win that big cup again.

APPENDIX I

THE MATCH REPORT
ST JOHNSTONE 2, DUNDEE UNITED 0
PERTHSHIRE ADVERTISER, 20 MAY 2014
BY GORDON BANNERMAN

IT STARTED ONE summer's night in Trondheim. And it ended on Cloud Nine in Glasgow's East End.

The most momentous season in St Johnstone's 130-year history was capped by the Perth club's first ever national trophy win, paving the way to a Saturday night party like no other in the Fair City.

From Peter Grant in 1919 to Steve Lomas last season, 23 managers came and went without seeing the club's name engraved on world football's oldest trophy.

The letter J had never been required by the engravers – until now, in Tommy Wright's first year in command. As anticipated, it was Saint Steven's Day. Unexpectedly, it wasn't all about May 17.

More than 15,000 ecstatic Perth supporters, many lured from across the world to see history in the making, savoured a day they will never forget, with goals from Steven Anderson and Steven MacLean eclipsing their Tayside rivals, who failed to penetrate the Perth defence for the fourth game in succession.

Both scorers, like their manager Wright, have emerged from dark days and hospital wards. It was another tactical masterclass from the man from Ballyclare. Some of the pre-match mind games had been worthy of José Mourinho.

And, crucially, his players delivered in textbook fashion with the opener, from testimonial man and former United player Anderson, fashioned on the training ground.

His back post header found the net from a David Wotherspoon corner as United keeper Radoslaw Cierzniak grasped at fresh air.

And a two-day party got going in earnest minutes from the end as the blue and white segment of Celtic Park erupted in unbridled joy when MacLean ensured the cup was coming to Perth.

His initial shot was blocked by Cierzniak after he pounced on the break of the ball off a United defender when Stevie May bullied his way forward.

The attacker and keeper were both grounded but MacLean showed the presence of mind and poaching instincts to roll the ball into the empty net and kick start celebrations which had been in the making for more than a century. Off came the shirt and he was into the crowd, knowing the game was up for United.

Rewind and the afternoon began to a backdrop of pyrotechnics and Celtic drummers, with the famous silverware paraded 15 minutes before kick-off by Saints legend Roddy Grant and Amanda Kopel, widow of United star Frank, who passed away recently.

Then vast banners bearing the badges of the rival Tayside clubs were raised aloft by hot air balloons promoting sponsors William Hill, with blue and white banners including one from Ballyclare, the modest home town of the St Johnstone manager.

The record-breaking Perth support may have been outnumbered two to one in a stadium awash with a spectacular blue and tangerine card display and swirling scarves minutes before kick-off, but before the full-time whistle, the road and the miles to Dundee beckoned for United fans doing a disappearing act.

In the second minute, keeper Alan Mannus gave notice of a nervous afternoon when he spilled a cross under pressure.

Only a flying Cierzniak save denied James Dunne from 20 yards in the 13th minute after Chris Millar released Brian Easton on the left flank. The cross squirmed off MacLean and Wotherspoon before the midfielder's pure strike demanded a spectacular touch over the bar.

Cierzniak got lucky in the 21st minute after a May free-kick crashed into the wall and the ball fell to Wotherspoon. The midfielder cut inside but his low shot was deflected by Gavin Gunning straight to his relieved goalkeeper.

But it was Saints' turn to get off the hook in the 27th minute when Dunne attempted to mop up in the Perth penalty box only for his clearance bid to strike Frazer Wright's arm at point-blank range and Mannus pounced before United could exploit the chaos.

In the 32nd minute, the width of the post denied United when Ryan Dow clipped a teasing Andrew Robertson cross towards goal, only for it to hit the upright.

Into stoppage time and Anderson rose to head home Wotherspoon's hanging corner at the back post in a mirror image of a recent strike at McDiarmid.

He became just the second St Johnstone player to score in a cup final, emulating Canadian international Nick Dasovic in the League Cup final of 1998.

Minutes after the restart, Nadir Ciftci floated a delicious free-kick over the wall. It clattered the crossbar and struck a stranded Mannus but somehow didn't trundle over the line after striking the prone keeper. In the 52nd minute, Saints fans and May were celebrating what they thought was another goal but, amidst the bedlam, referee Craig Thomson chalked it off and booked the striker for punching the ball over the line.

Minutes later Wotherspoon almost conjured up a classic solo strike after a weaving run and mesmerising footwork triggered by Michael O'Halloran's delicate flick inside his own half.

But the midfielder's rasping shot was parried by the keeper and within seconds Mannus was touching a Robertson effort round the post at the other end.

United sub Brian Graham and then Ciftci came perilously close to an equaliser, but the history of St Johnstone FC was being hastily updated when MacLean sealed their most famous win.

APPENDIX II

THE VIEW FROM THE STANDS
THE CELEBRITIES

COLIN MCCREDIE, ACTOR
TEARS OF JOY

MY SCOTTISH CUP default setting was formed at Muirton Park on Valentine's Day 1981. From that moment – a last-minute looping header by the late Ian Redford for Rangers that broke my eight-year-old heart – all the way to Jody Morris' penalty shoot-out miss at Hampden in the 2008 semi-final, Saints and the Scottish Cup only meant one thing: glory in defeat.

Of course, my personal 30 years of agony were nothing compared to the club's century of Scottish Cup failure. It was part of our psyche. Like many Saints fans, I genuinely believed I'd never wake up on a sunny May Saturday to find our wee team gracing the mighty Scottish Cup Final. My envy at seeing other wee clubs have their day in the sun made it even more unbearable.

That is until one day in April at Ibrox in 2014 in the shape of a long haired lad from Newburgh. Three touches later and the ball was in the net. As Stevie May spiralled away to celebrate, the legend on the back of his shirt was surely prophetic: May 17.

And then 23 minutes later Stevie May did it again and unbelievably we were finally in a Scottish Cup Final. Maybe, just maybe...

Simply reaching the final felt enough for me, reward enough after all the years of heartbreak. Although the stars were aligning,

I confess I didn't think we could actually win it – as poor Tommy Wright learnt a week before the final, when I was placed next to him at a club do, and I bored him with my anxiety.

As Tommy made his escape, he leant over and confided: 'You need to stop bloody worrying – we're going to win it. Trust me.' And so I did. And Wright was right. Destiny! May 17! Plus our record that season against Dundee United.

Fast forward to Celtic Park standing with my eight- year-old daughter, Maisie, and my best pals among 15,000 Saints fans – electric! Now was the time and now was the hour – and do you know what? It was torture.

The realisation of what was at stake and how close we were crippled me with fear. I endured 84 minutes of hell, even as 'Ando' rose at the back post to put us one up. Even as we rode our luck and the woodwork saved us. Not until Steven MacLean slid in with six minutes to go and the ball rolled towards the net in slow motion, did I know it was going to be alright. We were going to do it – we were going to win the Scottish Cup.

It felt amazing, 130 years of failure gone in an instant. My wee team had done it. We'd gone and won the bloody, proper Scottish Cup! And I was crying buckets. That release of anxiety, the pride in my club's achievement and the fact we'd persevered for so long meant so much to me and the thousands around me. As Dave Mackay hoisted that famous old trophy high above his head, we were for once truly glorious in victory! And it felt brilliant.

A FEW DAYS after we won the cup I made the decision that neither time nor fading memory would ever separate me from the moment we won the cup. So, I gathered together all the precious photographs of the day and arranged them into a giant poster. It now hangs with pride in my kitchen, the greatest day in St Johnstone's history framed as a permanent reminder of triumph.

At the heart of the poster is a giant photograph of my wee boy, Jack, wearing a blue and white jester's hat being kissed by my partner, Shirani, who is wearing blue and white extensions in her hair. They are smiling up at the massed ranks of Saints fans and behind them is the disappearing wall of tangerine as Dundee United fans fade from the stadium. What a day to go to your first-ever Saints game?

Below the family is a photo of my mate Mike Mason, who grew up with me in Letham and has supported Saints through thin and thin. A few days before the final we drove up from Glasgow to soak up the atmosphere around the town, buying cup final cup-cakes, eating blue rice at Pete Chan's Chinese take away and swapping good luck handshakes with everyone we met. On our journey we stopped off at the Bee Bar in Methven Street and I took a picture of Mike kneeling next to a giant flag which read "Good Luck Saints from all at The Bee Bar." He claims to hate being photographed and yet this is his favourite photo.

Next to Mike at the Bee Bar is the photo of an unknown fan I snapped walking to the game, emblazoned on his back is the date May 17. That day forever etched in history. There are three other pictures, all personal, but important to mention. One is a photograph of me in a blue hoodie holding Jack on my shoulders the way my dad used to hold me at Muirton Park in the days when winning the cup was the stuff of childhood fantasy. Next to that is a picture of the Saints young team resplendent in bucket hats, casual gear and holding a blue flare alight above their heads. It's an image I really cherish, proof that we have future fans and that our story will live on. Adults can often be hypocritical about young fans and their behaviour. I love the photo as it says 'we are young, we are Saints and we are buzzing.' Those are feelings we all had – in our own ways – on our date with destiny.

The final image is one I am enormously proud of. It was taken off stage the day after the cup final on that historic day when the cup was paraded through Perth. Jack is in my arms holding the cup, Dave Mackay is trying to wrestle it away from him and our manager, Tommy Wright, who had been so honest about the loss of his own son, is looking on at the fun we are having. I cannot begin to imagine what we were all thinking, but a warm sense of love washes over the entire picture and implicitly it is a love for St Johnstone and what they had just achieved on 'Our Day in May'.

GROWING UP IN Pitlochry, I've always been a St Johnstone supporter since I was a young girl and into my teenage years. I had been to many of their games, including some of the bigger matches. I remember us losing the League Cup final to Rangers in 1998 and recall Nick Dasovic's goal. We had all our faces painted that day at Celtic Park. The last few years I've probably been to a few more games and I don't think I've actually seen Saints lose during that time, which has been good!

I've made the rest of the girls in my curling team Saints fans. They are from all over Scotland, like Stranraer, Lockerbie and Glasgow, but are now adopted Saints supporters! I know quite a lot of the players, they train in Stirling as well, so I see them a lot, as well as other people who work at the club and support them. It's great the people who put in so much time for the club.

We fully deserved the semi-final win over Aberdeen. We were playing well as a team and when things are going your way it's hard to stop any team. We seemed to have great momentum in the second half. The atmosphere was great, as the Saints fans made a lot of noise that day.

It was a friendly final against Dundee United. It was a nice atmosphere amongst the supporters, which added to the day. We were in hospitality with the Saints fans and it was fantastic. I went with the rest of the girls and I'll never forget how nervous so many people were – so many people live for the club and want to see them do well. One of my main memories was seeing (TV presenter) Lorraine Kelly, as she is a die-hard Dundee United supporter and was dressed fully in orange. But I didn't see her at the end!

It was the best time to score just before half-time with Steven Anderson's header, and the worst time to lose a goal. It was good to finish that half on a high which I think made a big difference for the team. Both goals in the final came at the right time. For St Johnstone and for Perth, it was massive. It was simply an amazing day and we'll always have that cup final win.

APPENDIX III

THE VIEW FROM THE STANDS

THE FAR-FLUNG TRAVELLER: PART 1

JOHN WALKER

I LIVE IN Tuktoyaktuk, in the remote Northwest Territories in Canada. It's at the end of an Arctic Circle route favoured by the Ice Road Truckers. I'm 75 years old and I work at the local detachment as a civilian guard, but I'm originally from Perth where I was a tradesman.

When I first came to Canada, I had to rely on finding a place that sold overseas newspapers and I would get the Sunday Post on a Tuesday so I could get the Saints score. Once the internet arrived, things changed!

Regardless of miles and expense, I simply had to cheer on the Saints in the Scottish Cup final for the chance to witness history. All told, we had 22 take offs and landings, and the distance covered in my round trip was over 20,000 kilometres. Devotion is probably the word!

My journey began with a half-hour flight on a tiny plane from my home in frozen Tuktoyaktuk to Inuvik. That was just the first in a series of flights via Norman Wells, Yellowknife, Edmonton and a near five-hour journey to Toronto, before an Atlantic crossing with my son Ryan, 22, who made his first trip to Scotland.

I crossed three different time zones before I even left Canada! We were an hour late into Edmonton and the pilot said something about huskies chasing the plane down the runway. The trip cost approximately $8,000, but was it worth it? Yes, as nothing could beat the feeling!

When Saints got to the semis, I thought about coming over but didn't want to jinx them. But when Stevie May did the business against Aberdeen, there was no stopping me.

I always enjoy coming back to Perth every few years, but this time was special. We were there the week before the game and there was a buzz about the town I hadn't felt before. I grew up following Saints in their Muirton Park days and the first game I went to was with my dad to see us play Preston North End in a friendly. It must have been around 1947/48.

I relied on my long-time pal and retired Perth plumber Alex 'Shiner' McDonald to bag me a precious ticket for the final. I did an interview on STV the week before the game and had said I was quietly confident when asked about Saints' chances. On the Friday night, I had the pleasure of meeting fans in the Saints Club on Barossa Street and flags of our adopted countries were put up on the walls.

On the cup final day, we headed to catch the ex-Servicemen's bus and I really enjoyed the banter. We stopped at the Shettleston club for lunch, chatted to some United fans and then it was onto the game. We couldn't believe the mass of blue and white when we entered the stadium! Over 15,000 Saints fans from near and far – what a support, and the display of flags was unbelievable.

To win it was incredible, being there to see Saints finally do it having followed them for so long. Witnessing it with my son and 'Shiner' made it extra special. Even though we got on the wrong bus for our way back to Perth, and did another small marathon of a trip, we didn't care.

THE FAR-FLUNG TRAVELLER: PART II
BILLY INGLIS

I LEFT PERTH to carve out a career in Australia in 1986 and had returned to the Fair City just once for a family holiday in the intervening years – but I had to see my beloved Saints in a final!

I grew up in Letham, Hillyland and North Muirton and attended Our Ladies' and St Columba's, following Saints religiously in my youth. I'm 50 now, living in Melbourne, working as a factory supervisor for an air conditioning company.

I married a Perth lass, Cathrine, before emigrating and I had only managed to come home once, in 2008, when we brought our family of three girls for a holiday.

Fortunately for me, Saints had managed to qualify for the Scottish Cup semi-final and I went to the game where we lost to Rangers on penalties. What I do remember from that game was the wave of elation when we scored to go one up in extra time (scored by an Aussie, Daniel McBreen), mixed with the overwhelming horror and panic at the thought of not being able to go to the final, as I was already nearing the end of a six-week break.

It all came flooding back while watching the Aberdeen semi-final at Ibrox on my own in the living room late on a Sunday night. Once we equalised, unfortunately for my sleeping family, the volume got cranked up – by me not the telly! When Stevie May scored the second so near the end I knew that was it, but I paced back and forward kicking every ball, shouting at the ref for the final whistle. When it blew, I couldn't believe it, I was jumping up and down, yelling and screaming 'we've done it, we've done it'.

Then, almost like before, a wave of panic came over me again. 'Oh no, what am I going to do now?' I was not long in a new job and only had a wee bit of money saved up towards a planned holiday home to Scotland with Cathrine the following year.

As the texts and Facebook messages of congratulations started flooding in, with the added question 'are you going?' Cathrine told me 'I think you should go, we'll postpone the holiday until later.' She's heaven sent that girl! Someone asked me how I would feel if I went all that way and Saints were beaten – but my response was how would I feel if I didn't go all that way and they won? That would have been worse, much worse.

I got the time agreed off work and then trawled the internet for flights from Melbourne to Doha, onto London then Edinburgh. Total distance 17,800 kilometres!

I still have lots of family and friends in Scotland and I wanted to soak in all the build-up, as I had dreamt of the day all my life. I had seen plenty of other smaller teams do it, reach a Scottish Cup final, and wondered if we ever would.

In the end, I could never have imagined it would go so well. The emotions were flying out of me. I was remembering the hard yards put in watching the team at Muirton and now we have a Scottish Cup win. It was amazing, the trip of a lifetime.

It was worth every penny. I would have paid it 10-fold. What a time I had, from the minute I arrived – memories to last a lifetime. It means so much to so many people. I'm not sure the players realise what they have done. It means everything to us, the fans.

THE REUNION
STUART WOODS

The Scottish Cup final was the first match my dad, Mike, and I had attended together in over 15 years. We had been season ticket holders for about 10 years throughout the 1990s, enjoying both home and many away matches, travelling with the Auchterarder Supporters' Club. One of those, in particular, was the Scottish Cup semi-final defeat to Dundee United in 1991.

As my father and I both live outside of Scotland now, him in Sweden and me in the south of England, our visit began the day before when we both met at Edinburgh Airport and travelled to the home of my sister, Katie, in Dundee, whose partner, Gordon, happened to be a United fan and was also going to the match — not with us might I add! On the morning of the Cup final, it was an early start as we travelled through to Perth to meet my cousin, Chris, who had booked us on a bus leaving from the Scone Arms.

My father and I have always been St Johnstone fans, but having lived away for many years there was apprehension as to how we would feel watching the team play again. But as we walked into the stadium and saw the mass of supporters, as well as a few old familiar faces, our memories and feelings for the club came flooding back.

The match was amazing. Steven Anderson's goal came at the perfect time. It gave us time to soak up the atmosphere and draw breath for the very tense second half. Steven MacLean's goal helped, but it wasn't until that final whistle that we could completely breathe properly! I glanced at my dad at the end and neither of us could quite believe it. Even though he will deny it now, he was close to tears. The next half hour was just a big party in the stadium, which was fantastic. We loved it and will never ever forget it. I'd like to thank the players and everyone involved at St Johnstone Football Club for giving me these memories with my dad at my side.

Afterwards, it was celebration time, back to Perth and a quick visit to the Twa Tams before setting off back to my sister's in Dundee. It was a wrench leaving Perth that night, but family called. They were already out, so we had no time to change out of our Saints gear and it was straight to Frew's Bar. It isn't very far away from Tannadice and it may as well be painted orange! So we zipped our jackets up and headed in, but thought it wouldn't be busy after their defeat – wrong! It was full of United fans but, to be fair, everyone was pleased for us and we had a cracking night in the company of the losing supporters celebrating St Johnstone's Scottish Cup win. As stories go, it's one I'll never tire of retelling.

AUTOGRAPHS

AUTOGRAPHS

AUTOGRAPHS